Dutch Touches

Recipes and Traditions

Silver paneled bowl made by Gerrit Onckelbag, 1691 – 1732.
Bequest of Miss Charlotte A. Van Cortlandt. Museum of the City of New York.

by Carol Van Klompenburg and Dorothy Crum

*Associate editors: Miriam Canter, Jean Caris-Osland,
Joan Liffring-Zug, Juanita Loven,
Dana Lumby, Robin Ouren, Jane Pesek*

Penfield
Press

Dutch Touches *is a revised and expanded version of two previous publications,* Delightfully Dutch *and* Dutch Treats, *originally compiled by Carol Van Klompenburg. In addition to the many contributors noted throughout the book, we thank the following for their help as consultants, translators, or advisors on the earlier books as well as this edition: Dr. Philip Webber and Mina Baker-Roelofs, Central College, Pella, Iowa; Robert and Teresa De Jager, Maurice Birdsall, and Martha Lautenbach, Pella; Ann Kiewel, Director, The Holland Museum, and Margaret Wolffensperger-Kleis, Grace Antoon, Jaap R. de Biecourt, and Willard C. Wichers, Holland, Michigan; Olga Burgerhout Tipton, Cultural Affairs, Consulate General of the Netherlands, Chicago, Illinois; Harriet Rusticus, Assistant, Consulate of the Netherlands, Grand Rapids, Michigan; Cory Reed, Albany County Convention and Visitors Bureau, and Beverlee E. Forrest, Historic Cherry Hill, Albany, New York; Rich Goring, Crailo State Historic Site, Rensselaer, New York; Barbara W. Stankowski, The Holland Society of New York; John-Peter Hayden, Museum of the City of New York; Stephen Barto, Staten Island Historical Society, Staten Island, New York; Nancy Dana Gold, Sleepy Hollow Restorations, Tarrytown, New York; Olive M. Clearwater, Kingston, New York; Willa Skinner, Fishkill, New York; George Berndt, Martin Van Buren National Historic Site, and Sally A. Bottiggi, Columbia County Historical Society, Kinderhook, New York; Bill Alrich, Radnor, Pennsylvania; W.Z. Shetter, Indiana University, Bloomington, Indiana; Dorothy Neil and Kim Curry, Oak Harbor, Whidbey Island, Washington; Martin Meerma, Chamber of Commerce, Fulton, Illinois; Wanda Corn, Stanford University, Stanford, California; David F. Wiebe, Hillsboro Historical Society and Museum, Hillsboro, Kansas; Cedar Grove Chamber of Commerce and Harland and Marian Hopeman, Dutch Crust Bakery, Cedar Grove, Wisconsin; Arnold Koekoek, Dordt College, Sioux Center, Iowa; Carl Vandermuelen, Middleburg Press, Orange City, Iowa, and Dover Press.*

Recipe contributors are acknowledged with individual recipes as they appeared in original publications of Delightfully Dutch, 1984, *and* Dutch Treats, 1987.

Front cover: Tulips in the gardens of the Scholte Museum, Pella, Iowa. Back cover: Klompen Dancers, Tulip Time in Holland, Michigan. Photographs by Joan Liffring-Zug.

Graphic design by Esther Feske, Albuquerque, New Mexico; Diane Heusinkveld and Dana Lumby, Iowa City, Iowa.

Books by mail: Postpaid (prices subject to change)

> *Dutch Touches* $14.95
> *Dutch Proverbs* $10.95
> *Dandy Dutch Recipes* (Stocking Stuffer) $6.95

Write to Penfield Press, 215 Brown Street, Iowa City, Iowa 52245. Please send $2 for complete catalog.

©Penfield Press 1996. All rights reserved. Illustrations and text may not be reproduced without written approval of Penfield Press, except as part of a review of the book. ISBN 1-57216-024-1 Library of Congress Catalog Number 96-67373

Contents

About the authors:

Carol Addink Van Klompenburg, who is 100 percent Dutch, has written, co-authored, or ghost-written ten books. She lives in Pella, Iowa, with her husband Marlo and their three sons. During her childhood in Orange City, Iowa, she celebrated her Dutch heritage each year in that city's annual Tulip Festival. Now she and her family don Dutch costumes and scrub streets at Pella's annual Tulip Time. Carol graduated *summa cum laude* from Dordt College in Sioux Center, Iowa, a school with strong ties to the Dutch Reformed religious heritage. She holds a master's degree from the University of Minnesota and has taught writing classes at Dordt College and Central College in Pella.

Marvin R. Hiemstra, who traces his pure Dutch descent back to 1426, was born in Pella, Iowa. He received a Bachelor of Arts in Honors for Creative Writing from the State University of Iowa, now the University of Iowa, and a Master of Arts in Victorian Literature and Folklore from Indiana University, Bloomington. A member of the Academy of American Poets, The Poetry Society of America, and the Dramatists' Guild, Marvin is currently associated with the international award winning fine arts group, Juniper Von Phitzer Press. Author of eighteen books, he has created nine collections of poetry, including *Dream Tees* which was nominated for the Pulitzer Prize in Poetry. Each year Marvin performs his poetry and humorous prose across the United States and Europe. His work, *In Deepest U.S.A.*, is recorded on compact disk.

Dorothy Crum, editor, attended Ottumwa Heights Academy and Junior College, and received a B.A. degree in English Education from Marycrest College, Davenport, Iowa. After additional work at Drake University, Des Moines, and five years teaching high school English and Journalism, she worked as a state director for teenage groups for the YWCA in Iowa, and as a Health Educator for the Iowa State Department of Health. After marriage to Don Crum and moving to Iowa City, she became a full-time volunteer and mother of two children. She currently works as a freelance editor, and has been a long-time friend and associate of Penfield Press.

Other contributors: Harriet Heusinkveld, Pella, Iowa; Margaret Wolffensperger-Kleis, Holland, Michigan; Marilyn Newmeyer, Lancaster, California; Dorothy Neil, Oak Harbor, Washington, and Dennis Visser, Iowa City, Iowa, note their ties with Dutch culture and heritage in individual essays.

THE NETHERLANDS

National Boundary
Provincial Boundary
Canals
Rivers
Sea and Surge Barriers
★ National Capitals
◯ Major Cities
Neighboring Nations
IJsselmeer
Reclamation

0 5 10   20 Kilometers
0 5 10   20   30 Miles

WEST FRISIAN ISLANDS

GRONINGEN

Leeuwarden

Groningen

Waddenzee

FRIESLAND

DRENTHE

NORTH
SEA

Zuiderzee

IJsselmeer

projected

Alkmaar

NORTH
HOLLAND

Haarlem

Amsterdam

Zwolle

OVERIJSSEL

Vecht

Almelo

Enschede

Apeldoorn

Leiden

Utrecht

GELDERLAND

IJsselrivier

The
Hague ★

SOUTH
HOLLAND

UTRECHT

Rijn

Arnhem

Delft

Waal

Rhine

Rotterdam

Dordrecht

Nijmegen

Maas

's-Hertogenbosch

Breda

NORTH BRABANT

WEST
GERMANY

ZEELAND

Eastern Schelde

Roosendaal

Tilburg

Eindhoven

Düsseldorf

Western Schelde

LIMBURG

Antwerp

Meuse

Cologne

BELGIUM

Brussels

Maastricht

Bonn ★

6

Skating Through
Dutch-American History

57 B.C.   Julius Caesar conquers the low countries of Europe, the start of the 400 years of Roman rule for what is now the Netherlands.

400–800   The Franks control the Netherlands. In 496 A.D., the Frankish King Chlodowech (Clovis) is converted to Christianity. Dike building begins in Friesland.

800–1000   The Vikings raid and plunder.

1000–1500   What became the Netherlands is composed of small, autonomous principalities and towns without loyalty to any higher political power.

1450–1550   This period in music history is called the "Age of the Netherlanders," with most of the important musical posts in Europe held by composers and musicians from central and southern Holland, Belgium, and northeastern France. The Mass, motet and chanson, all for voices, are the main forms of musical expression in the courts and churches.

1500–1558   The Netherlands and other low countries become part of the Great Burgundian Hapsburg Empire. In 1516, Duke Charles of Burgundy also becomes ruler of Spain, and the Netherlands comes under Spanish control.

1559–1584   Willem I of Orange and Nassau, the Prince of Orange, serves as the first *Stadholder* of the Netherlands. (*Stadholder*: literally, the holder of the city; in actuality, military leader of the Netherlands.)

1568   Under the leadership of King Willem I, the Eighty Years' War against Spain begins.

1594–1597   Willem Barents, Dutch navigator, discovered the Barents Sea, north of Russia. He was lost at sea in 1597, but meteorological data he gathered is still consulted today.

1602	The Netherlands combines several Dutch firms to create the Dutch East India Company, a stockholder-owned firm granted a monopoly for Dutch trade with South-East Asia.
1606	Dutch sea captain Willem Janszoon discovered New Holland, which is now Australia.
1609	Henry Hudson, in the third of his four voyages of exploration, and the only one financed by Dutch merchants, explores as far north as the present site of Albany, New York. The Hudson River is named for him.
1614	A small Dutch trading post is built near present day Albany. It is abandoned three years later.
1621	The Dutch West India Company is chartered, with powers similar to the Dutch East India Company, for trade with the New World and West Africa.

The Exploration
*Settlers, Indians, Peter Minuit, and Peter Stuyvesant, Manhattan in
1617. Fort Orange, gabled houses and seventeenth century ships.*

By Chris Stoffel Overvoorde, Calvin College, Grand Rapids, Michigan.
Commissioned by the Dutch Immigrant Society for 1976 U.S. Bicentennial.

1624	A Dutch settlement called Fort Orange is started near the present site of Albany.
1625	A Dutch settlement begins on Manhattan Island. Peter Minuit, hired by the Dutch West India Company as governor of the New Netherland, names the village New Amsterdam.
1626	Peter Minuit buys the island of Manhattan from the Indians for $25 worth of European goods. The Dutch West India Company offers large land grants (patroonships) to those who settle fifty or more people in the new colony within four years.
1630	Village of Beverwyck is founded at the present site of Albany. It is later merged with Fort Orange.
1648	As a part of the Peace of Westphalia, the Netherlands signs a treaty with Spain ending the Eighty Years' War. The Netherlands is recognized as an Independent Republic of the United Provinces.
1652	The initial colony at the Cape of Good Hope (Africa) was founded by the Dutch East India Company, which wanted a port where ships could take on fuel, water, and provisions enroute to the Far East. About thirty-five years later, the Dutch were joined by the Huguenots. Later, when Napoleon overran the Netherlands, Britain sent troups to keep the Cape out of French hands and was awarded the colony. The Netherlands was a major colonial power until the Second World War, but after 1945 the colonies quickly became independent.

Coffee

Coffee shrubs grew in the wild in the Ethiopia-Arabia area. The Dutch began cultivating the crop in the East Indies, and the first coffee from Java reached Holland in 1712. For the next century, coffee was the most important crop in the East Indies. "I'll take a cup of java" was heard as "java" became an expression for coffee.

American Eden

In 1661, immigrant Jacob Steendam wrote of New Netherland:

It is the land where milk and honey flow;
Where plants distilling perfume grow;
Where Aaron's rod with budding blossoms blow;
A very Eden.

1664	The English, with four warships as a show of naval force, take New Netherland. Beverwyck is renamed Albany, and New Amsterdam is named New York in honor of the Duke of York and Albany, who later becomes King James II.
1673	A Dutch naval force recaptures New Netherland, but in less than a year the government gives it back to England for English backing of Dutch claims to Surinam (Dutch Guiana) in South America, whose export trade is valuable.
1782	The United States, with its Revolutionary War nearing an end, and the Netherlands sign a Treaty of Amity and Commerce, beginning the longest peaceful relations the United States has enjoyed with any nation. The treaty paves the way for a series of Dutch loans totaling $12 million to the struggling colonies, loans that contributed greatly to the success of an independent United States.
1795–1813	The Netherlands, weakened by a century of intermittent wars with England and France, falls to French invasion, and Napoleon names his brother Louis as King of the Republic. The Netherlands became independent again after the collapse of the Napoleonic Empire in 1813.
1814	Under the Congress of Vienna, Holland and Belgium become the United Kingdom of the Netherlands under King Willem I, but Belgium later revolts.
1830	Southern Netherlands secedes and forms the country of Belgium. Willem I recognizes Belgian independence, giving the Netherlands its present-day form.

The Midwest Migration
*American Revolutionary War soldiers: John Paulding, who caught a
British spy; Peter Ganzevoort, who defended Fort Schuyler, and
President Martin Van Buren. The painting also pictures four clergy-
men who were leaders of the migration to the Midwest: Albertus van
Raalte (Holland, Michigan), Cornelius van der Meulen (Zeeland,
Michigan), Hendrik P. Scholte (Pella, Iowa), and Father Johannes
van den Broek (Wisconsin settlements). With them are early settlers.*

By Chris Stoffel Overvoorde, Calvin College, Grand Rapids, Michigan.
Commissioned by the Dutch Immigrant Society for 1976 U.S. Bicentennial.

1834	Father van den Broek is sent as a missionary priest to the Fox River Valley in Wisconsin. Eventually 40,000 Dutch Catholics immigrate to the region, becoming the largest group of Dutch Catholics in the U.S.
1847	Albertus C. Van Raalte founds a colony in Holland, Michigan, and Hendrik P. Scholte founds Pella, Iowa. Their moves begin a wave of Dutch immigration to the United States.

Dutch Americans

Dutch settlers have been arriving in America since 1614. Today the
number of U.S. citizens descended from Dutch immigrants is esti-
mated at between 8 and 10 million.

Tragedy on Lake Michigan

In 1847, the "Phoenix," a ship loaded with immigrants, sank in Lake Michigan ten miles from Sheboygan, Wisconsin. Those aboard included 200 Dutch headed for new homes in Wisconsin. Only forty-two or forty-three passengers survived. Some of them reached shore in leaky lifeboats, using wooden shoes for oars.

1870   Holland, Iowa, later renamed Orange City, is founded as Henry Hospers organizes a committee to colonize northwest Iowa, where land is more available and less expensive than in his hometown of Pella.

1894–1896   Crop failures in the Dakotas and Montana cause Dutch farmers to move to Washington state. Lynden, the largest of the Washington settlements, begins in 1896.

1898   With the death of her father, King Willem II, Queen Wilhelmina begins her fifty-year reign, the first of three generations of women to rule the Netherlands. She abdicated in 1948 and was followed by her daughter Juliana. Queen Juliana abdicated in April 1980 and was succeeded by her eldest daughter, the present Queen Beatrix.

1927   The Netherlands begins a massive dike-building program to enclose the Zuider Zee. The project is completed in five years, and the Zuider Zee is transformed into an inland sea, which gradually became a freshwater lake, the IJsselmeer.

Skating or boating, anyone?

In the Netherlands, there are more than one-hundred lakes all linked by rivers and canals.

1929   To commemorate its Dutch heritage, Holland, Michigan, initiates an annual Tulip Festival in May. Other tulip festivals in Pella and Orange City, Iowa, were first held in 1936, and Albany, New York, started its annual festival in 1949. See "Tulip Bloom and Bust" for other Dutch-American celebrations.

1940–1945   The Netherlands remained neutral during the First World War (1914-18), though not without difficulty. It continued to pursue a policy of strict neutrality during the Second World War but was nevertheless attacked and invaded by Germany in 1940 and occupied for five years. Anne Frank writes her famous diary. Important dikes are destroyed. At war's end, another wave of Dutch immigration begins. Many settle in California.

The Great Migration
Depicts old and new immigrants who have made significant contributions to their adopted homeland including: President Theodore Roosevelt; World War II Generals J.A. van Fleet, Hoyt S. Vandenberg, Alexander Vandergrift, and writers Hendrik Van Loon, Pearl Buck, David and Meinert De Jong, Mark and Carl Van Doren, Jan De Hartog, Peter De Vries, Frederick Manfred. Through their works, the writers expressed the hopes and beliefs of all immigrants.

By Chris Stoffel Overvoorde, Calvin College, Grand Rapids, Michigan.
Commissioned by the Dutch Immigrant Society for 1976 U.S. Bicentennial.

1953	The United States Refugee Relief Act allows 17,000 Dutch to immigrate in addition to the regular 3,136 Netherlands quota. In 1958, the Walter Pastore Act allows an additional 8,900 Indonesian Dutch, expelled by Sukarno, to immigrate. By 1960, 50,000 Indonesian Dutch immigrated to the United States, many of them settling in California.

California Touches

Many California businesses reflect the Dutch influence and citizenry. Bellflower's newspaper is the *Holland News*. In Lakewood, a bowling center is named Dutch Village, the Artesia Bakery sells Dutch baked goods. The Northridge radio station, KCSN, broadcasts Dutch music, with special attention to listener requests.

Mile-High Dutch

Denver, Colorado's first Dutch Festival drew more than 15,000 visitors in June of 1983. The event was in a newly constructed Dutch Village, including a 40-foot windmill, on the campus of the Bethesda Hospital. The festival became an annual celebration of heritage of Denver's Dutch Americans.

1982	The Netherlands and the United States observe the 200th anniversary of the Treaty of Amity and Commerce. Queen Beatrix and Prince Claus tour the United States, address Congress, and attend events coast-to-coast.
1991	On November 14, the U.S. Congress and President George Bush proclaimed November 16 as Dutch American Heritage Day. Through House Joint Resolution 177, Congress designated this day to recognize Dutch Americans who have played key roles in the economic, social and political life of the United States of America.

Perseverance

Place two Dutchmen in a room and they will found a debating society; gather three Dutchmen together in a room, and they will found either a church or a political party.

The Integration
Twentieth century contributions of the Dutch are symbolized in this painting showing the forty-nine Bells of Gratitude Carillon in Meridian Hill Park, Washington, D.C., presented by the people of the Netherlands after World War II, Flags of War, the United Nations, flag of NATO, Brandenburg Gate, Mount Rushmore, and seals of colleges. Individuals portrayed include: President Franklin D. Roosevelt, Arthur Vandenberg, Piet Mondrian, Willem de Kooning, Jack Lousma, and Drs. William J. Kolff, Frits Wendt, R.J. VanderGraaff, Peter J.W. De Buy, and James Van Allen.

By Chris Stoffel Overvoorde, Calvin College, Grand Rapids, Michigan.
Commissioned by the Dutch Immigrant Society for 1976 U.S. Bicentennial.

About Liberty

In love of liberty and in defense of it, Holland has been our example.

— Benjamin Franklin

Newspapers

The first Dutch-language newspaper in the United States was *De Sheboygan Nieuwsbode*, started in 1851. By the beginning of World War I, there were twenty-five Dutch-language newspapers and magazines in the U.S.

15

About Frugality

The trouble with the Dutch is that they offer too little and demand too much. — Lord Chesterfield

Kolf and Klootschieten to the New World?

Back in the fourteenth century, many Dutch people played *kolf* with rubber or spun wool balls and a stick with a curved end. Golf, a sport taking up a much larger playing area, is supposed to have come from *kolf* and is played according to the same principle. Another version was played on ice in the winter with a club resembling a hockey stick and a leather-covered ball the size of a grapefruit. Sample equipment is preserved at the Wassenaar Golf Club just north of The Hague in the Netherlands.

Klootschieten, another traditional sport, is still played in the east of the Netherlands and just over the German border in Westphalia. It is similar in one aspect to golf, in that the obstacles are in the natural terrain of the playing area. The difference is that a wooden ball weighted with lead is thrown over a distance of several kilometers. Teams of ten pitchers take turns at throwing.

A 1628 copper engraving shows Dutch children in a school playground playing a game resembling present-day baseball. Some historians maintain that Dutch emigrants took the original form of baseball with them to America in the seventeenth century.

A Debt of Gratitude

It is said that the American bride-to-be who is showered with gifts before her marriage owes a debt of gratitude to a stubborn little Dutch girl. According to legend, the girl's father refused her a dowry because she insisted on marrying a miller, her true love, rather than the farmer he had chosen for her. They married and lost the dowry, but their friends, seeing their plight, sought to make up for it with what became the first bridal shower, "raining" china, linen, pots and pans and other household goods on the young couple.

From: *The Dutch Book: Celebrating 100 Years on Whidbey Island* by Dorothy Neil, Oak Harbor, Washington

Photo courtesy of the Consulate General of the Netherlands.

The Royal family, H.M. Queen Beatrix and H.R.M.
Prince Klaus of the Netherlands and their sons.

Modern Holland in Brief

The Netherlands is a gem among the European countries — small, beautiful and many-faceted. From a soggy landscape, the industrious Dutch have built one of Europe's most progressive countries. More than any other people, they have literally built their country with their bare hands, grain by grain of sand.[1] The process of claiming the land from the water has never stopped. This industry has created much of the 15,770 square miles that is now the Netherlands, which measures less than 200 miles from tip to toe (including its seven northern islands). With only 100 miles between the beaches of the North Sea to the west and the wooded Dutch/German border to the east, it is, by comparison, barely bigger than the thumb on the mitten-shaped state of Michigan.

[1] From "The Quality of Life in The Netherlands." Ministry of Economic Affairs, The Netherlands. 1992.

The name Holland originally referred to only two of the country's western provinces, but has become accepted as an alternate name for the entire country. The official name, the Netherlands, means, appropriately, the lowlands.

Its three largest cities are Amsterdam, Rotterdam, and The Hague. The twelve provinces are: North Holland, South Holland, Groningen, Friesland, Drente, Overijssel, Gelderland, Utrecht, Zeeland, North Brabant, Limburg, and Flevoland. Current population is over 15 million. Dutch is the first language, however, Frisian is a second language in the province of Friesland.

The Netherlands is a constitutional monarchy with a parliamentary system. Queen Beatrix is head of state, but the power is wielded by the prime minister, the cabinet, and the parliament. The seat of government is in The Hague, but Amsterdam is the capital city. One of the festive highlights in the capital city is the April 30 celebration of Queen Beatrix's official birthday. For this national holiday, trade laws are lifted and budding retailers set themselves up in a colorful market place. Revellers abound in a celebration of nationality.

Days of Orange

On royal birthdays and other important days for the House of Orange, life is brighter. A *wimpel* (fringed orange banner) flies above the Dutch flag. In some villages, children wear an orange *sjerp* (sash) draped over the left shoulder and tied at the right waistline. A splash of orange is in order for the day.

Orange sprinkles decorate rusks and breads. Some cooks bake a special *oranje koek* (orange cake).

Thoroughly Done

Studying a miniature recreation of New Amsterdam at the Museum of the City of New York, Prince Bernhard of the Netherlands asked: "Are any of these buildings still standing?"

Louis Auchincloss, then museum president, said: "I had to reply, 'None.'"

The prince shrugged and smiled: "You do things very thoroughly in New York."

From: *The City of New York* by Jerry E. Patterson.
Harry N. Abrams, Inc., New York.

William and Mary

Many Americans know that Queens Wilhelmina, Juliana, and Beatrix, sovereigns of the Netherlands in this century, are descendants of the House of Orange-Nassau, as was Willem (William) I, who served from 1559 to 1584 as the first Stadholder (military leader) of the Netherlands.

Less well known is that from 1689 to 1702, all Americans, English, and Dutch were under the same sovereign or leader, therefore in one sense, members of closely related nations.

King William III and Queen Mary II ruled England and the American Colonies as joint sovereigns, and William was hereditary Stadholder of the Netherlands. William III was a great-grandson of Willem (William) I. He was also the great-grandson of a French king, a Scottish king and a Medici princess, and the grandson of an English king. Mary II was the daughter of King James II of England.

The House of Orange-Nassau was so named because the family land holdings were in Nassau in west central Germany and in Orange in southern France, as well as in the Netherlands.

William and Mary were held in general esteem. In New York, with its many Dutch settlers, there was special affection for "Dutch William." Use of their names, and of Nassau and Orange, in America usually honors these monarchs.

The College of William and Mary (1693), where Thomas Jefferson, James Monroe, and John Marshall were educated, is in Williamsburg, Virginia. The first building of Princeton University, completed in 1756, was named Nassau Hall. The Continental Congress met there in 1783. Contrary to the suggestion in the name, the Colony of Maryland was named for Queen Henrietta Maria, wife of King Charles I of England.

Queen Mary II died in 1694 at the age of thirty-two. King William III died in 1702, at age fifty-two.

Royal Reflections

Juliana

Queen Juliana came to visit a
campus —
  which shall go unnamed.
The professors in caps and gowns
  lined the sidewalks,
  an honor guard,
while the College President
escorted
  the Queen and Prince Bernhard
into the chapel for a convocation.

An elderly professor,
  too deaf to know how loud he
  talked,
broke the solemn stillness
  by announcing to nobody in
  particular:
"Wat heeft zij tog dikke benen!"
("What fat legs she's got!")
Everybody heard him.
Queen Juliana too.

She stopped in from of him,
smiled,
and said with an arch of
playfulness:
*"Mijnheer, daar moet het hele
Oranjehuis op rusten."*
("Sir, these legs need to hold up
the whole House of Orange.")
Everyone in earshot cheered.

No question about it,
the old professor lacked style
but nobody minded
because Queen Juliana had such
class.

From Style and Class *by Sietze Buning.*
© *Middleburg Press. Orange City, Iowa. 1982.*

Wilhelmina

Queen Wilhelmina
was entertaining the Frisian
  Cattle Breeders' Association
at dinner.

The Frisian farmers
didn't know what to make of
  their finger bowls.
They drank them down.

The stylish courtiers from The
Hague nudged each other
and pointed
  and laughed
at such lack of style.

Until the queen herself
without a smile
raised her finger bowl
  and drained it
obliging all the courtiers to
follow suit
without a smile.

The courtiers had style
but Queen Wilhelmina had class.

Claiming the Land

Dutch Canals

by Marvin R. Hiemstra

It is often said, "God made the Dutch, the Dutch made the canals, but the canals made Holland."

When the first Germanic tribes wandered into the area which is now called the Netherlands, it was almost uninhabitable. The area was composed of huge lakes — stormy as seas — marshes and low thickets, deep bays that carried fierce northern storms into the heart of the country, and rivers that constantly shifted and flooded because the incline was not adequate to allow the rivers to flow into the ocean. The first inhabitants created mounds of earth, as best they could, upon which they lived precariously by fishing, hunting, and collecting the eggs of sea birds.

Throughout the centuries, the lakes, the rivers, and the ocean caused horrendous catastrophes: both loss of life and constant loss of tillable land.

The Dutch carefully surrounded the lakes and marshes with dikes. Windmills, putting suction-pumps into motion, poured the water into canals which conducted it into the rivers and toward the sea. Between 1500 and 1858, more than 900,000 acres of fertile land were created in the former lake and marsh areas. Work continues and slowly, but surely, *Ijsselmeer* (the Zuider Zee) is being transformed into top quality farmland.

The path of the rivers was carefully regulated and divided to control and disperse the enormous mass of water into nondestructive flow patterns.

Much of the Netherlands is lower than sea level so a monumental system of dikes — huge bulwarks of earth, wood, granite, and metal — creates an artificial, yet effective, coastline to protect the country from the ocean. Windmills and various mechanical pumping systems remove rainwater and the water that constantly oozes from the earth — pumping it into the canals which move it out to sea, except at high tide when the gigantic locks on the

21

mouths of the rivers must be shut to restrain the tremendous force of the ocean.

The whole country is covered with a network of canals which irrigate the land and are, at the same time, highways for the people. The towns communicate with the sea by means of the canals; canals lead from town to town, binding the towns to the villages, and uniting the villages. Smaller canals surround the farms, the fields, and the kitchen gardens, taking the place of walls and hedges. Every house is a little port. Ships, barges, boats, and rafts sail through the villages; wind round the houses, and navigate the country in all directions.

Only after World War II and the world-wide proliferation of autos did Holland create a complete network of highways.

Holland was developed to be navigated by canal. The enlightened visitor should take to the water whenever possible to enjoy and understand the Netherlands as it was created. Dutch architecture, for example, was designed to be the most visually effective when viewed from the water. Seen from the water, Dutch buildings are magnificent, indeed.

The initial settlers in Pella, Iowa, were delighted to discover that canals might be possible in Iowa. They soon realized that canals would not be necessary because of the fortuitous layout of the rivers and the anticipated appearance of the railroads.

Currently, as part of an excellent, long-range Dutch architecture and environment plan, Pella is installing a picturesque Dutch canal in its famous downtown Dutch Front area.

Law of the Dikes

"Dike or leave," the Frisians used to say. They meant that a Friesland farmer was expected to maintain his section of the dike perfectly, or he would be asked to leave. If a farmer decided to give up his land, he threw his spade into his section of the dike. Whoever pulled the spade from the ground and cared for the dike became the new owner of the land. Whenever a dike was in danger, immediate "dike peace" was in effect. All quarrels were forgotten.

Windmill Island in Holland, Michigan contains this sluice gate to control the water level of the Black River to protect the dikes. Similar gates are found throughout the Netherlands to control flood waters.

The Finger and the Dike

Plug a hole in a dike with your finger — hydraulically impossible. But in fiction and legend, anything can happen. Nineteenth-century American writer Mary Mapes Dodge penned *Hans Brinker, or The Silver Skates*, the tale of a Dutch boy who plugged a dike with his finger.

The legendary boy hero and the story became world famous. The Dutch town of Spaarndam built a monument to the character Hans Brinker, to honor the courage of Dutch youth through the centuries. The monument is a popular tourist stop for Americans.

Working with the Wind and the Land

Windmills

More than half the nation of Holland is below sea level, and the fight to reclaim land from the sea was already underway when the Romans arrived. Sometimes the sea won, flooding the countryside and killing thousands, but the Dutch always pushed it back again with their massive dike building and land drainage.

On a typically breezy day in 1282, a thrifty North Brabant carpenter found a way to put the winds to work. He fastened a slatted cross to the roof of a building, tied a sailcloth to the wings and connected it to a wooden wheel with troughs. The power of the wind turned the wheel, and dumped water from his land to the other side of the dike.

Many Hollanders followed his example, using wind power to drain water from their land. Half the present land area of the country has been reclaimed from the sea through the system of dikes (which would reach from New York to Chicago) and draining of the land.

Windmill power was also used to saw wood, extract oils from nuts and seeds, grind wheat, and to make paper, glue, mustard, snuff, and fabric.

Wherever Dutchmen lived, mills sprang up. In 1640, two wheat-grinding windmills overlooked the Hudson River. Early settlers in Holland, Michigan built windmills for sawing wood and grinding grain.

Seeking to hinder foreign industrial competition, the Netherlands passed a law in 1750 forbidding the export of windmills. Later it even refused to issue passports to Dutch millwrights.

Over time, a windmill language developed. If the wings were in a vertical-horizontal position, the mill was open for business. If they were at a 45-degree angle, forming an X, the mill would not run for some time. Wings just before (clockwise) the horizontal-vertical position indicated mourning. Streamers, flags, baskets and hearts were strung from the wings on special occasions such as weddings and at Whitsuntide.

Eventually, windmill power lost out to gasoline and electric

24

power. In the nineteenth century, there were 9,000 windmills in Holland; today there are only 900, with only 300 still in operation. A windmill preservation society has been organized to buy and restore old mills that are offered for sale.

Even though the sea has, through the centuries, been a potential enemy for the Dutch, it is also a valuable resource. Fishing and shipping provide many jobs for this tiny country with the highest population density in the world — 1,000 people per square mile. Thirty percent of all the European Economic Community exports pass through Dutch seaports. Rotterdam is the busiest port in the world.

Others work the land (polders) reclaimed from the sea growing vegetables and flowers, or raising fodder for dairy cows.

Windmill Lore

A sense that justice will prevail is contained in the proverb, "God's mills grind slowly, but surely."

The windmill is an important part of Dutch history, and as such has become an integral part of Dutch culture in the form of proverbs and folk sayings. As a warning that one may have to face the consequences of his actions, the Dutch say, "Be careful or you'll have to face the wind." Cautious people are said to wait with a decision until they know out of which corner the wind is blowing. Seizing an opportunity is known as pumping while the wind blows.

When someone seems a little daffy, he is said to have been hit by a mill, or when someone's business is not doing well, the Dutch say, "He cannot keep his mill going."

Netherlands
A Country of Many Costumes

by Carol Van Klompenburg

Over the centuries, instead of developing a national costume, the Netherlands has been a country of many local costumes. In the sixteenth century, many Dutch villages and islands were isolated from each other, and their residents chose their own clothing traditions and styles. Developing over decades and centuries, these costumes gave expression to a sense of local community.

In 1805 an Amsterdam publisher, Maaskamp, sent reporters throughout the country to record the dress of Dutch men and women. After he received their descriptions, he commented, "The Netherlands are a small piece of ground which have a greater diversity of clothing than almost all the continents outside Europe....Amsterdam alone has almost as many different costumes as districts: every town in Holland has its own."

Different costumes often reflected local occupations. In Urk and Volendam, for example, where fishing was the primary occupation, the men wore clothes which were warm, roomy, waterproof and windproof. The silk stockings and knee breeches of the nobility had no appeal to them.

Dress also reflected the economic conditions of an area. In the more prosperous Zeeland, Holland, and Friesland provinces, women wore a great deal of elaborate gold jewelry. In Drenthe and Braabant, however, such ornamentation remained very simple.

Local costumes could also reflect their wearers' rank, sex, and marital status. The clothing of noble families and clergy was different from that of the farmers, fishers, and crafts people. In Flevoland a small black circle at the back of a hat indicated a woman was of marriageable age.

When local costumes began to develop in the sixteenth century, women's clothing was composed of six items: a linen chemise, skirt, apron, kerchief, *kroplap* (bib), and cap.

Five basic cap styles are the foundation for the many varieties found in local costumes: *hul, luifelmuts, floddermuts* or *keuvel, bolvormige zak* and *kornet*. In Marken, the hat developed twelve

26

different components, including bands, embroidered ribbons, lace, cardboard, and *baize* (red fabric). The *baize* was thought to ease rheumatism and gout. Marken women put the hat on only once each week, and they slept in it, in a half-seated position.

In Zeeland, if the huge hat was angular, its wearer was Catholic. If pressed into a rounded shaped, its wearer was Protestant.

Under their caps, Dutch women wore an *oorizjer* (metal casque). In North Holland, if a farmer's wife wore a golden casque, area residents could be sure her barn held forty or more cows. If her casque was silver, her barn held at least twenty-five.

In the nineteenth century, wearing local costumes peaked in the Netherlands, as in the rest of Europe. At the beginning of the twentieth century, the custom began to wane.

In the Netherlands today, local costumes are still common in Marken, Staphorst, and Volendam. There is only a smattering of them in other villages, where they are worn primarily by older women.

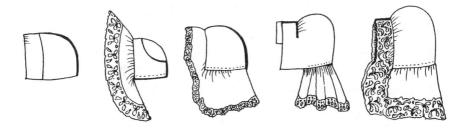

Drawings above from left to right show various types of Dutch caps: Hul, Luifelmuts, Floddermuts, Kornet, and Bolvormige Zak.

Illustrations by Diane Heusinkveld.

Klomp, Klomp, Klompen

Wooden shoes, or *klompen* as the Dutch call them, began as inexpensive and practical footwear for farmers and fishermen. Carved by their wearers, they kept feet dry and were good insulation.

Each Netherlands province developed a slightly different shoe style with its own decoration. The use of wooden shoes in the Netherlands declined in this century until the 1970s, when city residents began using them as practical wear for washing the car or working in the garden.

About 8,000,000 a year are made by the wooden shoe factories in the Netherlands. In the United States, there are two factories at Holland, Michigan, and one at Orange City, Iowa. Their shoes are worn by costumed dancers and other participants at Dutch celebrations, and are a popular souvenir item.

Wooden Shoe Comfort

In 1897, the *Island Times* of Coupeville, Washington, reported: "We have a shoe factory here…only fifty cents a pair; warranted to fit and give good satisfaction. If one has a good quality toe corn, there will be a place made for it where it will have room to grow without getting pinched." Farmers put a handful of hay in their wooden shoes for increased comfort. The hay produced a cushion.

From: *The Dutch Book: Celebrating 100 Years on Whidbey Island*
by Dorothy Neil, Oak Harbor, Washington

Dutch Art

by Virginia A. Myers

A windmill, a dike, and tulips in the foreground create a neat and tranquil scene that is unequivocally Dutch. These are outward manifestations. Caesar found a sea-land of "mystery and fear," with the most ferocious fighters he had encountered anywhere, a people who saw resistance hopeless, yet refused to submit. In Charlemagne's time, "churches were built on artificial hills and bishops went about in boats." In 1282 a sudden terrible ocean flooded much of the ancient land.

Rijksmuseum. Detail from "Fleurs et fruits."

Tulip by Jan van Huysum (1682-1749).

Fifteen-thousand people were drowned and the Zuider Zee replaced a small lake.

Coping with the arduous problems of wrestling the land from the sea, the Dutch learned many lessons from invaders. A Roman general named Drusus built dikes and embankments to protect his armies. He dug canals so that his ships might pass from river to river without having to venture into the dangerous North Sea.

Against this background of natural calamity and regular incursions by outsiders, the Dutch people emerged and reemerged with renewed courage and creative powers. In the fifteenth century the Van Eyck brothers left an indelible mark on the origins of oil painting. Hieronymous Bosch followed with his moralistic allegory paintings, especially "The Garden of Earthly Delights." While he was thought of as the most medieval painter of the fifteenth century, he also injected a subjective, individualist expression into paintings which could not have been made at an earlier date and which placed him in the category of "modern" painter.

It was not until the seventeenth century that a sense of Dutch

29

nationality was realized in the arts. Copper plate etching reached a zenith in the hands of Rembrandt. His paintings were imbued with a deep sense of mood and inward meaning which continues to influence artists to this day.

The Rembrandthuis, where the artist lived and worked, is a long walk from the Rijksmuseum in Amsterdam. Open to the public, this home of the artist contains his wooden printing presses and a nearly complete collection of his etchings on permanent display. Rembrandt's son Titus was born there, and his wife Saskia died in the home. After twenty years, due to his indebtedness and bankruptcy, he was forced to leave the house in 1659. "Night Watch" by Rembrandt and other masterpieces are in the Rijksmuseum, repository of the greatest collection of Dutch art in the world.

Frans Hals, Jacob van Ruysdael and Jan Vermeer created cherished works with a serenity and intimacy that have given Dutch painting of this period a readily identifiable character. Hals painted his famous group portraits with posing laughing noblemen; Ruysdael his melancholy but amiable landscapes depicting dramatic skies, water and windmills; Vermeer his familiar quiet interiors. Anecdotal paintings of ice-skating scenes, taverns and ships were created by scores of Dutch artists to satisfy the demands of an affluent middle class who decorated their homes with original works of art.

Today Vincent Van Gogh, one of the greatest painters of the nineteenth century, continues to be the idol of many students attending art schools. His life story and tortured landscapes seem to carry poignant messages to sensitive young artists who seek their own place in history.

In the twentieth century, Piet Mondrian organized the Dutch de Stijl group, a movement which emphasized painting abstract geometric shapes. The Dutch immigrant to America, William de Kooning, is noted for being one of several artists working in the New York School who gave abstract expressionism an identifiable form in the early 1950s.

Many museums in America contain outstanding Dutch paintings and prints.

—Virginia A. Myers is a professor in
the School of Art and Art History
at the University of Iowa.

Delftware

Throughout the world, Dutch Delftware is recognized by its blue and white color. Blue decoration on opaque white, with a luminous beauty, is standard, but some Delftware is multicolored, and some original Delft may have been brown and white.

Delftware was first made in seventeenth-century Netherlands in the style of imported Oriental porcelain. It takes its name from the town of Delft, where the finest Royal Delft porcelain is still painted by hand at the Porceleyne Fles. A single piece of new, authentic Delftware may sell for $3,000; antique pieces may cost much more.

Manufactured, contemporary patterns of delftware, in a variety of quality and price, can be found in several Dutch towns and cities. One is Holland, Michigan, at De Klomp Wooden Shoe and Delft Factory.

Dutch Folk Art Hindeloopen

Hindeloopen, the art of decorating wooden furniture and other wood utensils, began in the Dutch village of Hindeloopen as a poor man's way of decorating. Hindeloopen sailors may have seen Norwegian folk painting (rosemaling) on their voyages; this, combined with the influence of Indonesian designs acquired during their travels, inspired this folk art style.

Traditional background colors are brick red, dark green, and muted blue. Favorite motifs are flowers, scrollwork, and sometimes birds.

A number of professional artists still practice this traditional folk art. Sallie Haugen DeReus of Pella, Iowa, introduced Hindeloopen painting to the United States in the mid-1970s.

Plate Talk

Collection at the Historical Village, Pella, Iowa.

*Another man's burden
is easiest to bear.*

*As the clock ticks at home,
it ticks nowhere else.*

From sowing comes mowing.

Hurrah! We are still alive.

*The early dawn has
gold in its mouth.*

After rain comes sunshine.

A Great Time in the Netherlands

by Marvin R. Hiemstra

I have visited Holland many times and enjoyed the country more each trip. For anyone planning a trip, here are a few suggestions about making the most of your visit.

1) Sit down and list your interests: food, architecture, music, scientific achievement, art, or whatever. Whatever you name, you'll find fantastic examples in Holland.

2) Purchase a recent date guidebook to Holland and highlight what interests you. When you finish, skim back through and you'll know exactly what you want to see.

3) Plan your trip to focus on three or four locations in Holland: areas with the most interest for you. Decide on lodgings at a central location and train or drive out from there each day. Train service is excellent, fun, and takes you to the center of everything.

Holland is a tiny country. Don't waste time and energy with any unnecessary change of lodging. Use your time to discover and enjoy the country.

Almost every town center — large or small — boasts a Dutch VVV *(Vereniging voor Vreemdelingenverkeer)*, Tourist Information Office. The staff, who speak English well, as do most Dutch people, will help you find a good place to stay in any price range, even cordial lodging in a private home, and will give you information about an incredible variety of events and places to visit. VVV has a multitude of maps and guide sheets: take a short self-guided house walk in an older district and you will be amazed at the practicality and the beauty of the Dutch lifestyle.

4) If possible, travel to Holland in the autumn, the sight of colored leaves reflected in a canal is breathtaking; or the winter, usually mild with intriguing holiday customs; or the spring, the blossoms are unsurpassed. Avoid summer when heat and swarms of tourists can be less than delightful.

Here is a very brief summary of an ideal trip focused on just three locations: Amsterdam, Haarlem, and Delta Expo. You will probably fly into Amsterdam, a good central place for lodging. If possible, stay in the Leidseplein area; it is exciting, convenient, and pleasant. The many elegant attractions of Amsterdam are well-known. I will give you just a short list of my favorites:

- Take two glass-topped canal boat excursions: One during the day and one at night. This is the very best way to enjoy and understand the design of Amsterdam.
- Visit the Maritime Museum, Scheepsvaartmuseum, a monumental 1656 structure. Magnificently presented — you will discover how the Dutch ingeniously mastered the world of the sea.
- Indonesian food is the best food in the city. I've never been in an unsatisfactory Indonesian restaurant. My current favorite is Sama Sebo, P.C. Hooftstraat, very near the Rijksmuseum. Order a small Rijsttafel, rice table with several spicy dishes, and don't forget the splendid dessert, coconut ice cream frozen in half a coconut shell.
- Enjoy the Rijksmuseum — Rembrandt's "The Night Watch," other resplendent paintings, and other subject areas of this huge museum are all superb — and the neighborhood just north across the water, Singel Gracht, and Nieuwe Spiegel Straat, where antique shops of every type abound, and all the little side streets are jammed with picturesque dwellings.
- Spend evenings at Muziektheater or Concertgebouw or the Rembrantsplein clubs and cabarets, or all three, depending on your interests.

Haarlem, only about fifteen minutes from Amsterdam by train, is a magnificent locale. Without the bustle of a big city, one steps happily into the Dutch past. The old part of Haarlem is a small area filled with interest.

- Grote Markt, one of the best town squares in Europe, is surrounded by splendid buildings, including the Church of St. Bavo with its world famous Muller organ of 1738, which Mozart enjoyed playing when he was ten.
- The Frans Hals Museum fills a gracious 1608 alms-house surrounding a beautifully restored seventeenth-century garden — one cannot say which is more vibrant, the art or the setting.

• Teylers Museum is a state of the art museum of science built in 1778 and magnificently frozen in time. The stunning Age of Enlightenment architecture, the immense and beautifully crafted scientific instruments of the period, the superb fossil collection, and drawings by Rembrandt, Raphael, and Michelangelo, make this — the oldest museum in Holland — a true delight.

• If you are in Haarlem between the end of March and the end of May, visit the seventy acre Keukenhof Gardens and/or the Frans Roozen show gardens and bulb field for an experience of color and beauty you will never forget.

Looking on your map of the Netherlands, you'll see that the Delta Works are about as far southwest as you can go in that country. A trip there is a very long day trip from Amsterdam, but it is worth every minute. You will need to make reservations, check with the VVV, whether you train down and take a special bus for the final distance, or drive down.

• You will have the privilege of observing the most extensive hydraulic engineering project in history. I visited in 1982 when "boxes" the size of immense skyscrapers were being dug in the ocean floor to hold the manmade coastline: concrete piers, 130 feet high, that hold movable steel barriers, 138 feet wide.

• Depending on the season, you may be able to take a fifty-minute boat trip near the Storm Barrier, or walk into the interior of one of the great concrete piers, or view the extensive and extremely interesting exhibits and the fantastic deltascape from the Exhibition Center roof.

This introduction to the interesting pleasures waiting for a visitor to Holland is only a hint of what you will discover if you plan your trip with care.

Tulip Bloom and Bust

The perfect tulip should have a tall stem; the flower should consist of six leaves, three within, and three without, the former being larger than the latter. Their bottom should be proportioned to their top; their upper part should be rounded off, and not terminated in a point. The leaves, when opened, should neither turn inward nor bend outward, but rather stand erect; the flower should be of middling size, neither over-large nor too small. The stripes should be small and regular, arising quite from the bottom of the flower. The chives (stamens) should not be yellow but of a brown color.

— from *Dr. Samuel Johnson's Dictionary*
6th Edition, 1785

History relates that for one rare tulip bulb, an eager Dutch merchant once traded two loads of wheat, four loads of rye, four oxen, four pigs, twelve sheep, two barrels of wine, four barrels of beer, two casks of butter, 1,000 pounds of cheese, a bed, a suit, and a silver mug.

That supposed bargaining was in the early 1630s, about fifty years after tulips were introduced into Holland from Turkey. Tulips were an immediate hit. No well-to-do burgher of good taste could be without tulips. Prices skyrocketed, especially for exotic varieties. People thought the tulip craze would last forever.

The bubble burst in 1634. Dutchmen who had mortgaged homes, estates, and industries to buy tulips were selling them at 5 to 15 percent of costs. Fortunes were lost, and it was years before this aspect of the economy recovered.

The Dutch never lost their love for the tulip, however. It has remained a Dutch symbol, and people in the Netherlands and other growers have developed more than 2,000 varieties.

Tulip Festivals and Celebrations

In the merry month of May
When tulip blooms we touch,
At festivals we play;
It's colorful and Dutch.

Old Holland is transported to America through Dutch festivals and celebrations held annually throughout the country. Making these festivals a happy success are hundreds of willing volunteers, all of them sharing a spirit of fun, work, and heritage. For the thousands of visitors, the festivals are a spectacular show of spring at its best and offer pleasant reminders of Dutch contributions to America.

With the bloom of spring, there are annual Tulip Festivals at: Holland, Michigan; Pella, Iowa; Orange City, Iowa; Fulton, Illinois; Albany, New York; Skagit Valley, Washington, and at Hofstra University in Hempstead, New York.

Oak Harbor, Washington, celebrates "Holland Happening" each April. In June, Bethesda Hospital in Denver, Colorado sponsors a Dutch festival. In July, Cedar Grove, Wisconsin, schedules "Holland Days," and Edgerton, Minnesota, celebrates "Dutch Days." Grand Rapids, Michigan celebrates "Dutch Heritage Day" on November 16 with recognition ceremonies and special events. The Holland Society of the New Jersey and New York City area sponsors a "Blessing of the Ship" weekend in March and a "New Netherland Day" in September.

Ottawa, Ontario, Canada's "Festival of Spring," in mid-May, culminates with the splendor of the blooming of more than one million tulips presented to Ottawa by Queen Juliana of the Netherlands after she sought refuge there during World War II. The festival includes kite flying, races, markets, craft demonstrations, and tours of the flower beds.

Scrubbing the city streets is an important feature of Dutch celebrations. Above: Annual Tulip Festival in Orange City, Iowa.

Proper, Orderly and Clean

Deftig (proper) is a term respected by the Dutch. In the Netherlands, it is *deftig* to shake hands with all present, including children, when entering or leaving a home. Only when speaking to a social equal does a *deftig* person use first names. Going Dutch at restaurants is *deftig*. It is expected, unless different arrangements have been clearly stated in advance. Orderliness is a part of life, with a time and place for everything. Life is punctuated with regular coffee breaks. Housework is organized by days and hours.

In Dutch, the word *schoon* has two meanings: clean and beautiful. Saturday is *schoonmaakdag* (cleaning day). The Dutch are unmatched in their spotless housekeeping. The windows sparkle, and the sidewalks are scrubbed clean with soap and water. Each morning the bedding is hung from the windows to air. Visitors are expected to carefully wipe their feet upon entering a home. The annual *grote schoonmaak* (great cleaning) is the sole topic among traditional Dutch homemakers for two or three weeks each spring.

Courtesy Library of Congress.

This map of "Nowel Amsterdam en L'Amerique" is dated 1672.

Important Dutch Settlements
East Coast

Henry Hudson

English navigator, explorer Henry Hudson was hired in 1609 by the Dutch East India Company to find a northeast passage to the Pacific. He sailed the Dutch ship Half Moon westward, entering Chesapeake Bay, Delaware Bay, and later, New York Bay. He was the first white man to ascend the Hudson River, now named for him. Reports of profitable bartering with the Indians for valuable fur pelts gave the Dutch reason to claim the newly explored region located between the Delaware and Connecticut Rivers.

Still in search of a northern passage to the Orient, Hudson set sail in 1610 on what would be his final expedition. This voyage took him to Hudson Bay by way of the Hudson Strait. Forced to winter at Hudson Bay, his starved and diseased crew mutinied there in 1611, and set Hudson, his son, and seven men adrift in a small boat without food and water. Hudson was never seen again, but his legacy lives in the regions that bear his name.

Engraving ©1866 by Johnson, Fry & Company.
Reproduced from the Collections of the Library of Congress.

*Governor Stuyvesant destroying the summons
to surrender New Amsterdam.*

40

Peter Stuyvesant

History knows him as Peter Stuyvesant, but he always signed his name "Petrus," his given name. He was director-general of Curacao in the Dutch West Indies, where he lost a leg in naval action.

In 1647, when he was about fifty, Stuyvesant was sent by the Dutch West India Company to become the fourth governor of New Amsterdam, now New York City. Hot-tempered and dictatorial, he was immediately unpopular.

Stuyvesant was a rigid Calvinist member of the Dutch Reformed Church, in charge of a colony of around 1,000 including Dutch, English, Scandinavians, African slaves, and others. Stuyvesant refused to let the Lutherans organize a church, deported a Lutheran pastor, and used jail and whips against some of them, as well as the Catholics, Mennonites, Jews, and Quakers. Finally, the people appealed to the government of New Amsterdam, and Stuyvesant was ordered to honor the principles of religious freedom.

When the British demanded his surrender in 1664, Stuyvesant refused. With a garrison of barely one hundred fifty soldiers, a citizenry that did not choose to resist, and an eleven day blockade of supplies by the British, Stuyvesant conceded his office.

Nine years after Stuyvesant's surrender to the English, a Dutch fleet with 1,600 men recaptured New York, Albany, and other towns along the Hudson River. A letter to the Dutch government stated: "Recovery of this province will, in time, be able to confer...great profit and considerable advantage on the state of our beloved Fatherland."

Unfortunately, the Fatherland didn't see the potential of North America. Six months later the land was transferred back to the English to gain British recognition of Dutch rights to Surinam (Dutch Guiana) in South America. The Dutch government saw more potential in the slave and spice trade of that area than in the furs and farms of New York.

41

Albany, New York

Current capital city of New York, Albany is the oldest continuous settlement in the original thirteen colonies. A stopping off place for explorer Henry Hudson and his ship the *Halve Maen* (Half Moon) as he sought a northwest passage to the Orient, this area along the banks of the great river bearing his name was first established as a fur-trading post, Fort Orange, by the Dutch West India Company. Later in 1688, when the British drove out the Dutch, the settlement was granted a city charter and renamed for the Duke of Albany. The flavor of its rich heritage remains distinctively Dutch.

A spectacular proclamation of its Dutch origin is embodied in the nation's largest working weather vane, a two-ton copper replica of the Half Moon. The weather vane, which is six feet nine inches long by eight feet ten inches high, turns with the wind above the block-long State University Plaza. The Plaza is the headquarters of the State University of New York.

Albany has many landmarks that preserve its Dutch heritage. A Visitors Center located in Quackenbush square provides orientation and guides to the city's rich heritage and historic sites. The Albany Institute of History and Art, one of America's first museums, also provides an overview, including Dutch culture, of the area.

A site with special Dutch interest is the First Church (Reformed), dating from 1642. The present church was built in 1799, and has many artifacts and records from its earlier days. The pulpit was carved in Holland in 1656.

Schuyler Mansion State Historic Site is a 1761 Georgian brick house built by Philip Schuyler, Revolutionary War general and father-in-law of Alexander Hamilton.

Ten Broeck Mansion, home of the Albany County Historical Society, is a 1798 Federal-style brick house built by General Abraham Ten Broeck.

The New York State Library has a large collection of early Dutch manuscripts. A collection of the Albany Institute of History and Art includes Dutch artifacts, religious paintings, furnishings, ceramics and manuscripts.

Another colorful reminder of Dutch beginnings is the city's annual Tulip Festival in May. Tulips bloom in profusion, including

Neeefus Photographers

Historic Cherry Hill is a 1787 Georgian frame house in south Albany, where five generations of Van Rensselaers, descendants of the recipient of a 700,000 acre patroonship that extended along both sides of the Hudson, lived until 1963. It is now is a non-profit educational institution chartered by the New York State Department of Education. The interior is "as though the owners had stepped out for a minute." Displayed are antiques from two centuries including textiles, silver, and Oriental pieces acquired by a family member who was a missionary in China.

the "Orange Wonder," proclaimed by Queen Wilhelmina as the capital city's official flower. Festivities include street scrubbing, traditional Dutch costumes and wooden shoes, *Kinderkermis*, a children's fair, and *Pinksterfest* (*Pinkster* is Dutch for Pentecost) celebrating the city's mixed heritage. Activities include dancing, music, arts, crafts, foods, and theater. A highlight is the crowning of the Tulip Queen and her court.

Annual Tulip Festival, Albany, New York.

43

*Van Cortlandt Manor in Croton-on-Hudson tells the story of one of
New York state's earliest and most prominent families of Dutch descent.*

*Philipsburg Manor, Upper Mills in North Tarrytown, is a restoration of
an early Dutch farm and trading center with grist mill and barn.*

Photos courtesy of Sleepy Hollow Restorations, Tarrytown, New York.

Rensselaer, New York

Located across the Hudson from Albany in Rensselaer, is the Crailo State Historic Site operated by the state of New York. The museum is in a Dutch-style house built by Hendrick Van Rensselaer in 1704. Delftware, Hudson Valley sidechairs, other Dutch furnishings and decorative arts tell of early Dutch colonial history and culture. A slide show explains local Dutch architecture.

With advance reservations, groups may use the restored basement kitchen to prepare an entire meal, or perhaps, a simple spicy pound cake as it was done two-hundred or three-hundred years ago.

Other events include: In summer, there is a series of outdoor evening concerts. Each January 6, Crailo celebrates the merry Dutch holiday Twelfth Night, or *Drie Koningen*, an open house with refreshments beside a cozy fire, and music.

Tarrytown, New York

In Washington Irving's Sleepy Hollow country, Tarrytown, New York, stand the homes of two powerful Dutch immigrant families, Van Cortlandt Manor and Philipsburg Manor. Irving's home, Sunnyside, completes the trio of historic houses known as Sleepy Hollow Restorations.

Descendants of Stephanus Van Cortlandt occupied Van Cortlandt Manor from 1697 to 1945. In the manor house dining room, visitors may see delft biblical tiles original to the house. In addition to the manor house, visitors may tour the ferry house, where travelers on the old Albany Post Road were fed and housed, and the eighteenth-century gardens and orchards.

From the stone house and gristmill of Philipsburg Manor, Frederick Philipse managed his 52,000 acres. The land was sold at auction after his descendants backed the British in the American Revolution. Visitors can see also an eighteenth-century New World Dutch Barn.

Sunnyside was described by Washington Irving as "a little old-fashioned stone mansion, all made up of gabled ends, and as full of angles and corners as an old cocked hat." Sunnyside's paths and gardens were all planned by Irving.

Irving is best remembered for his stories of the Dutch. He is buried in the cemetery of the Old Dutch Church of Sleepy Hollow,

The Old Dutch Church of Sleepy Hollow, Tarrytown, New York, was built in 1697 by Frederick Philipse, First Lord of the Manor. It has been in use ever since, "except in Revolution."

past which schoolmaster Ichabod Crane fled in terror from the Headless Horseman in Irving's well-known story *The Legend of Sleepy Hollow*. Shadow puppet performances of *The Legend of Sleepy Hollow* are presented weekly at Sunnyside. Irving's *Rip Van Winkle* has been read by generations of American school children. His *A History of New York. ...by Diedrich Knickerbocker* is a satirical account of life in Dutch New York.

Kinderhook, New York

Kinderhook, too, features Washington Irving. The Luykas Van Alen House is a restoration museum of the Dutch architectural style. Its museum shop is the Ichabod Crane School House, named for the main character in *The Legend of Sleepy Hollow*. Irving modeled this character after Jesse Merwin, Kinderhook schoolmaster in the days when Irving was a tutor. Activities at the Luykas Van Alen House restoration include an antique festival in June and a farm day in August.

Kinderhook is rich in history. Legend says that Henry Hudson named it *"Kinderhoeck,"* Dutch for "Children's Corner," when Mohican children there came to see the vessel in which he was exploring.

President Martin Van Buren was born here. So was a legend, which says when Van Buren first used the term "O.K." in his 1836 campaign for the United States presidency, that it stood for "Old Kinderhook."

While serving as president, Martin Van Buren bought a Kinderhook mansion named "Kleinrood" and renamed it Lindenwald, as it is known today. Built in 1797 by Judge Peter Van Ness, President Martin Van Buren bought Lindenwald in 1839 from his life-long friend, the judge's son William P. Van

White House Collection, Washington, D.C.
Martin Van Buren, 1782-1862

Ness. Van Buren wrote that "Old Mr. Van Ness built as fine a House [*sic.*] here as any reasonable man could." He did not like William's many changes, tore them all down, and later wrote of his own son, Smith Thompson Van Buren, making "alterations without a stint...What nonsense."

The National Park Service administers Lindenwald and the surrounding Martin Van Buren National Historic Site.

President Martin Van Buren's home, Lindenwald, located in Kinderhook.

Photograph courtesy of Martin Van Buren National Historic Site, Kinderhook, New York, United States Department of the Interior.

The Luykas Van Alen House, built in 1737, is a fine example of rural Dutch architectural style. Located on Route 9-H in Kinderhook, New York.

Photograph courtesy of the Columbia County Historical Society.

Other historic sites at Kinderhook are operated by the Columbia County Historical Society. The James Vanderpoel House is called "The House of History." Activities there include an annual Christmas Greens Show the first weekend in December, and in May, an architectural elements show.

Photo courtesy of the New York State Office of Parks, Recreation and Historic Preservation, Palisades Region.

The Senate House State Historic Site, Kingston, New York.

Kingston, New York

Kingston was the first capital of New York. The first elected New York Senate met September 9, 1777, at the house of Abraham Van Gaasbeck. A month later, British troops landed at Kingston and all but one of the houses were gutted by fire. Their sturdy stone walls remained, however, and many were rebuilt, including the Van Gaasbeck house. Now known as the Senate House, it became a State Historic Site in 1887 and is open to the public.

The Old Dutch Church at Kingston was organized in 1659. Its guests have included George Washington and Netherlands' Queens Juliana and Beatrix. The present building, erected in 1852, retains a steeple bell that was cast in 1794.

Schenectady, New York

Schenectady was founded in 1661 by Dutchmen. Arendt Van Curler, nephew of Kiliaen Rensselaer, and fourteen others from Albany bought 128 square miles of land from the Indians.

Homes were built inside a stockade, or fence built of logs with

The Abraham Yates House (circa 1700) is an example of Colonial Dutch architecture in the Stockade District of Schenectady, New York.

a blockhouse at one corner. Farms were outside. On February 8 and 9, 1690, the stockade and all homes — about sixty — were burned in a massacre by 114 French and 96 Indians. Sixty residents were slain, twenty seven were taken captive. Others managed to escape, but some of them died in the bitter cold.

There are more than forty pre-Revolutionary structures in the stockade area with historic markers naming such early settlers as Abraham Fonda, Isaac Vrooman, Hendrick Brouwer, Adrian Van Slyck, Johannes Teller, and others. Many high Dutch gables and front *stoeps* can be seen on the annual "Stockade Walkabout" held the last Saturday in September. Some of the private homes are opened for tours. The Schenectady Historical Society is one of the sponsors.

Coxsackie, Fishkill, and Hurley, New York

The Bronck House Museum of the Greene County Historical Society at **Coxsackie** dates from 1663 with later additions and contains eighteenth- and nineteenth-century Dutch furnishings.

Built in 1731, the Dutch Reformed Church at **Fishkill** was used as a prison during the Revolutionary War. Trinity Episcopal Church at Fishkill served as a hospital for soldiers. A mile south of Fishkill is the Van Wyck Homestead Museum, owned and operated by the Fishkill Historical Society. In 1732, Cornelius Van Wyck built a three-room house that is now the east wing. Archaeological programs of the Society have led to discovery of thousands of artifacts relating to the Revolutionary War. The name Fishkill is derived from two Dutch words: *vis* and *kil*.

Each year on the second Saturday of July, some of the privately owned homes historically significant to the Dutch heritage of **Hurley** are opened to the public. Hurley is located near Kingston. The tour is sponsored by the Dutch Reformed Church.

Photograph by Anthony A. Lanza. Courtesy Staten Island Historical Society.

The Voorlezer's House.

Staten Island, New York

The Richmondtown Restoration on Staten Island, established by the Staten Island Historical Society and the City of New York, includes more than thirty buildings on one-hundred acres. The earliest buildings were erected by Dutch settlers.

Built before 1696, the Voorlezer's House is the earliest known elementary school building standing in the United States. The *voorlezer* was a lay minister and teacher of the Dutch Reformed Church.

51

New York's Brooklyn Museum

Model of the Jan Martense Schenck house, built about 1675.
Model built by Albert Fehrenbacher (1969).
Photos courtesy of the Brooklyn Museum, Brooklyn, New York.

Jan Martense Schenk came to America in about 1650 and operated a mill. The stone house which he built about 1675 remained in use until 1952, when it was dismantled and reconstructed at the Brooklyn Museum.

In the reconstruction, the house exterior was returned to its original appearance. The interior is furnished to show visitors the way of life of the early Dutch in America. The restoration was made possible through a gift of the Atlantic Gulf and Pacific Company.

The two-room house of seventeenth-century New York was commonly oriented to make the south room a combination kitchen, office, and main room. The view of the fireplace wall pictures furniture as it is believed it might have been arranged in the 1600s.

The south room was the kind of space referred to as a hall in early English documents. Museum literature identifies the large

The south room, a combination kitchen, office, and main room, of the Jan Martense Schenck house as reproduced at the Brooklyn Museum.

Another view of the south room of the Schenck House.
This kind of main room was called a hall in early English documents.

A portion of the north room of the Schenck House,
commonly the bedroom and parlor.

table that dominates the room as a continental example with a
frame of urn-shaped turnings and a plain slab top.

The north room was commonly the bedroom and parlor. The
rug on the table follows a Dutch practice brought to the New
World. The fireplace features tiles. There are two bedboxes, built-
in beds enclosed with doors or curtains. Silk curtains are used in
the Schenk house restoration.

Jersey City, New Jersey

As part of the initial colony of New Netherland, small colonies of
Dutch settlers were located on sites of present New Jersey. Cur-
rently, the Half Moon Visitors' Center, Holland Village in Liberty
State Park, Jersey City, provides information on the significance of
Dutch heritage in the area. Plans are underway for a New Nether-
land Museum to be located at Croton-on-the-Hudson, New York.
This will include an open-air museum of a seventeenth-century
Dutch Village.

Middle America

Iowa

Pella, Iowa — A Place of Refuge

Around the town square of Pella, Iowa, is an assortment of tiny shops with brick fronts and tiled, stair-stepped or gabled roofs. The shops are decorated with delft tile, Hindeloopen folk art and Dutch lace curtains.

Dutch pastries such as *banket* (almond roll) and *speculaas* (spice cookies) are favorites. Butcher shops feature Pella bologna, made according to a recipe brought by Dutch immigrants.

Arriving in 1847, *Dominee* (Rev.) Hendrik P. Scholte found one log cabin. In front of it, he placed a sign proclaiming "Pella," thus naming the new town for a city of refuge for early Christians in Asia Minor. Many of the 780 who arrived with Scholte had no time to build houses that first fall, so they built huts of straw or dug cellars and covered their dugouts with frames of sticks and long slough grass.

The area became known as *Strooijstadt* or Strawtown. That name has been retained by the Strawtown Inn, housed in a 130-year-old former home, which features lodging rooms and formal and informal dining in an Old World atmosphere.

The Scholte House, built by Rev. Scholte in 1848, remained in the family for four generations and was then donated to the town for use as a museum. Many of the original Scholte furnishings and memorabilia remain, along with the Lautenbach collection of antique Euro-

Replica of church built in 1855 by H.P. Scholte, Pella founder. The Latin words were his motto: "In God is our refuge and our strength." (Based on Psalm 46:1.) The church is in the Pella Historical Village.

pean furniture. The Scholte museum is open afternoons, March–December, and by appointment.

The Historical Village, a complex of 20 buildings, portrays the style of early Dutch immigrant life. Exhibits include the outstanding Birdsall antique delft collection, a working grist mill, and a miniature Dutch village. Village is open daily, April–December.

When Pella celebrates its Dutch heritage at the Tulip Time festival the second weekend in May, its streets and gardens abound with tulips, and thousands of its residents don Dutch costumes and wooden shoes.

Sinterklaas at Pella's Miniature Dutch Village in the Historical Village.

Queen Wilhelmina State Park, at Mena in western Arkansas, is the location of The Queen Wilhelmina Lodge. The first lodge, built in 1897 as a retreat for railroad passengers, was largely financed by Dutch interests, and was named in honor of the then young Queen Wilhelmina. The original lodge fell to ruin; a second was destroyed by fire, but the current modern construction offers an aura and elegance of days gone by.

Orange City, Iowa — The House of Orange

Orange City, Iowa, was first called Holland and was later renamed in honor of Dutch royalty — the House of Orange. It was founded in 1870 by settlers moving from Pella to find cheaper and more available land in northwest Iowa.

In 1936 residents founded a Tulip Festival, which became an annual event, except from 1942-1946 when it was interrupted by World War II. Festivities include parades, a flower show, an evening theatrical performance, horse-drawn trolley rides, and street dancing. A *Straatmarkt* simulates a Dutch open air market.

At left:
Members of "The Pride of Dutchmen Band" of the Maurice-Orange City High School wear Dutch costumes of red coats, black pants and wooden shoes.

Below, left:
Van Amsterdam boat float at the annual Tulip Festival, Orange City.

Below, right:
Northwestern State Bank, Orange City.

The Tulip Festival is celebrated the third weekend in May.

Other local attractions include the Century House and the Old Mill. Built at the turn of the century by Orange City's first mayor, the Century House has been restored to classic decor and houses area antiques.

The Old Mill was built by hand by Andrew Vogel, who also built a multi-million dollar business. It is open for tours year round. Vogel, a Dutch immigrant painter who didn't like the quality of paints available, started making his own. The Diamond-Vogel Company was the result.

A few blocks from the Old Mill is a 100-foot windmill which houses the Northwestern State Bank.

Nearby towns with sizable Dutch populations include Sioux Center, Hull, Rock Valley, Sheldon, and Hospers. Hospers is named for Henry Hospers who led the move from Pella to northwest Iowa. Hospers attracted other immigrants to the area by publishing a paper *De Volksvriend* (Little Friend of the People) in which he advertised the advantages of this new Dutch settlement.

When Hospers and the other Dutch settlers founded Orange City, they set aside one block for a public park, staked off lots, and laid aside one-fifth of the proceeds from the sale of those lots for a college fund. Twelve years later they founded Northwestern Classical Academy, now Northwestern College.

This fireplace with Delft tiles is inside the windmill built at Orange City by Andrew Vogel. Furnishings were imported from Holland. On the grounds of the Diamond-Vogel Paint Company, the windmill is open to the public.

Michigan

Holland, Michigan

The first Dutch settlement in Michigan was Holland. It was founded February 9, 1847, by the Reverend Albertus C. Van Raalte and
the first settlers. Within a few years, Dutch immigrants had started four villages nearby — Zeeland, Vriesland, Drenthe, and
Overisel — the first of a group of villages known as *De Kolonie*.

Today, Holland attracts visitors all year. There are two Dutch
theme parks, two wooden shoe factories, a spectacular Tulip Festival in May and a profusion of seasonal flowers.

At Holland's Dutch Village theme park are many features including an imported *draaiorgel* (street organ) and *zweefmolen* (circular swing), canals, and replicas of Dutch buildings, one of which
is a popular restaurant, the Queen's Inn. Visitors come to see *klompen* dancers, wooden shoe carving, farm animals and the reproduced Frisian farmhouse with attached barn and antique furnishings, museums and shops.
A unique attraction is the
"weigh-house," a replica of
the same structure in Oude-
water, Holland, where, in
the seventeenth and eigh-
teenth centuries, people ac-
cused of witchcraft were
brought to be weighed — if
you weighed too little for
your body structure it was
assumed that you were able
to fly, and therefore, a
witch. Other buildings feature typical gabled facades
and orange roof tiles im-
ported from the Nether-
lands. The shops offer a variety of imports from the
Netherlands and around
the world.

*The Queen's Inn Restaurant at Hol-
land's Dutch Village has a reed roof
constructed by a thatcher (rietdekker)
from the Netherlands; delft tile fire-
places, and huge ceiling beams inscribed with favorite Dutch proverbs.*

Tulip Time parade of infants, children and parents, Holland, Michigan.

Below: Building on Windmill Island representative of Marken Island.
These structures house shops, plus collections from Holland.

Windmill Island

The De Zwaan Windmill, tall as a twelve-story building, stands on Windmill Island Municipal Park in Holland, where canals, shops and exhibits are a reminder of the Netherlands. The 200-year-old windmill was moved in 1965 from Noord Brabant by special permission of the Dutch government. Graham flour ground by the windmill's power is available in the shops. Among the buildings on the island is a replica of a posthouse, a fourteenth-century Netherlands wayside inn, which features antique Dutch furnishings, documents, and memorabilia. Visitors can see also, on the canal, a reproduction of the drawbridge over the Amstel River at Ouderkerk, Noord Holland.

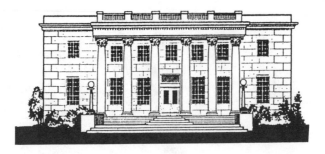

The Holland Museum is located in a landmark building and presents permanent and changing exhibits that reflect Dutch heritage and the history of the Holland, Michigan area.

The Holland Museum, formerly the Netherlands Museum, offers 400 years of Dutch heritage and 150 years of the Dutch in Holland, Michigan. Visitors enjoy permanent exhibits as well as changing exhibits. Some highlights of the permanent exhibits are: displays of delft and decorative arts, a replica of a Dutch fisherman's cottage, an 1860 Amsterdam doll house, eighteenth-century furniture, 1939 New York World's Fair displays, a hand crafted carousel, and historical reference material on such topics as "The Faces of Holland." Located in the beautiful Centennial park, the museum is open all year.

The Cappon House Museum, built in 1874, was the residence of Holland's first mayor, Isaac Cappon, a good Dutchman, and his family of sixteen children. Featured in the home are handcrafted woodwork, bronze hardware and original family furnishings.

The Cappon House Museum

The village of **Zeeland,** part of *De Kolonie*, sponsors a walking tour of architectural and historic sites. Many homes on the tour were built by Dutch immigrants of the mid-nineteenth century. The Zeeland Museum displays antiques from Zeeland's early history, including a display of dolls dressed in traditional costumes of the Netherlands provinces. The Hall of Pioneers records the story of the colonization of Zeeland.

Fred Oldemulders at the Original Wooden Shoe Factory
in Holland, Michigan.

The wooden shoe factories in Holland are tourist attractions as well as producers of shoes for sale, including most of those worn by the mile-long line of Holland Tulip Time *Klompen* dancers. The dancers, numbering almost 1,400, perform Dutch folk dances. Their costumes represent various provinces in the Netherlands.

Each spring, there is a brilliant display of over a million flowers at Veldheer's Tulip Gardens and Farm. On the grounds are three Dutch windmills and a canal. Visitors can see craftsmen carve wooden shoes at the DeKlomp Wooden Shoe factory, or potters and artists create delftware at the Delftware factory.

Grand Rapids, Michigan

Michigan's second largest city, famed for its publishing, arts, and furniture, has the highest percentage of Dutch ancestry of any American city. The central office of the Dutch International Society is located here, as well as a Consulate of the Netherlands. There are many businesses and establishments that reflect Dutch heritage. Dutch American Heritage Day is celebrated each November 16 with recognition ceremonies and other events.

Minnesota

Beginning in 1856, a married man could gain title to 160 acres of government land in southern Minnesota for $200, or $1.25 an acre. This opportunity brought the first Dutch settlers to Minnesota.

Greenleafton, a few miles from the southern border and about fifty miles west of the Mississippi River, was named for Anna Greenleaf of Philadelphia, who willed $4,000 to the Board of Domestic Missions of the Dutch Reformed Church of North America "for destitute portions of the west." Arriving in 1856, when Greenleafton was unbroken prairie land, were Derrick Alink, William Boland and their wives, and Aaron John Nagel. All had left Alto, Wisconsin, in three covered wagons drawn by oxen. The Boland's son George was born in the straw-covered wagon that was their home during the first winter.

Nearly all Dutch who came to Minnesota were farmers. Those who were Catholics joined with Belgian Catholics in settlements.

Edgerton, in southwest Minnesota, celebrates Dutch Days the third Tuesday and Wednesday of July. Stores create Dutch window displays, and events feature Dutch costumes and foods.

Some of the other Minnesota towns with significant populations of Dutch heritage include: **Hollandale, Hills, Jasper, Ghent, Minnesota, Clara City, Hancock, Brooten, St. Joseph, Sauk Rapids, St. Cloud, Onamia, Hinckley,** and **Sandstone.**

Illinois

Fulton, Illinois

In the days of steamboating, Fulton was a transfer and warehouse port between the upper and lower reaches of the Mississippi River. Lumbering, a big part of its historic past, attracted immigrants seeking to work the land. In celebration of a strong Dutch heritage, an annual Dutch Days Festival is held the first weekend in May. The festival features a parade with authentic Dutch costumes of all the provinces and *Sinterklaas,* street scrubbing, *klompen* dancing and *klompen* making, arts and crafts with Hindeloopen painting, Dutch foods, a Dutch Dress-A-Doll contest, tours and other events.

Wisconsin

Cedar Grove, Wisconsin

Settlement of this Dutch community was very small in the beginning. Local historians attribute this partially to the 1847 tragedy of the "Phoenix," a ship carrying over two-hundred immigrants, many of them Hollanders, that burned and sank north of Sheboygan, Wisconsin. On board, were families bound for the Cedar Grove area. Among the few survivors, were four daughters of the Schuppert family. Their parents and four brothers drowned in the disaster, but three of the sisters settled in the Cedar Grove area.

Many of the first Dutch settlers came from other settlements such as Holland, Michigan. They were engaged in farming, lumbering, and fishing. As these natural resources became depleted, many of the original settlers moved on to other territories, but Cedar Grove has continued to grow and prosper.

Cedar Grove celebrates its Dutch heritage each July with a Holland Festival. Among many activities and events are: street scrubbers, *klompen dansers* (wooden shoe dancers), wooden shoe races, a scenic bus tour, travelogue films of the Netherlands, a parade, a fashion show of Dutch costumes, arts and crafts, music, and Dutch foods. The area boasts the "World's Largest *Worstebroodje*" (pig-in-the-blanket).

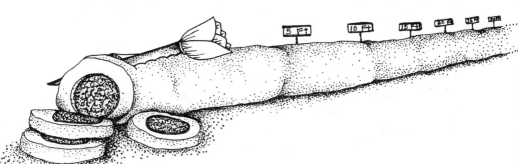

Illustration by Diane Heusinkveld.

A record-breaking 109-foot Worstebroodje *was created by Harland Hopeman, who, with his wife Marian, owns the Dutch Crust Bakery in Cedar Grove. Initially the recipe was adjusted, then proper baking tools especially made to handle five- or six-foot sections that are then connected. Proceeds from sales by the slice help support a group of* Klompen Dansers. *The Hopeman's daughter Heidi was a member of the group.*

Pacific Coast

Washington

Oak Harbor, Washington

Located on Whidbey Island, Oak Harbor had been "settled" for a number of years when Hollanders began to arrive. The first Hollander settlers came from earlier settlements in Michigan and the Dakotas. They were attracted to the Northwest by offers of land companies and the lure of fertile land. Oak Harbor resident, historian Dorothy Neil notes in her book *The Dutch Book, 1894-1994*, that one entrepreneur, extolling the virtues of the area, took some of the biggest potatoes ever seen and other vegetables to the Midwest to impress upon the Hollanders that whatever the hazards of a new settlement might be, they would never starve.

The little steamer "Idaho" brought its first Hollanders to North Whidbey in 1894. Eighteen colonists were aboard. Within two years, there were two-hundred industrious, thrifty Hollanders on North Whidbey, some with little or no money. One settler is said to have purchased a ticket in Holland, Michigan for "as far as it would take him." He had five dollars left when he arrived in Oak Harbor. Those who braved the prospect of a new settlement, cleared land, built cabins and began farming or working the timber trade. Churches, schools, and businesses were established. In the 1990s, fourth and fifth generations of the early day settlers of this community of 19,000, gather in coffee shops and bakeries for afternoon and morning coffees.

See a Dutch windmill and a Dutch boy street-sweeper statue in Oak Harbor's City Beach Park. Holland Gardens in Neil Park features a windmill and many varieties of tulips, daffodils and other summer and fall blooming flowers. Ramaley Memorial Park's tulip display brightens the "Dutch Village" in the spring. The Island County Museum contains historic reference to the Dutch, as well as the multi-cultural heritage of the area. The Orren and Ruth Ward Memorial Museum in the Neil Tower, features displays of cultural heritage. The Nydam farm, south of Oak Harbor, displays several dozen wooden shoes on the side of the barn, as well as a small windmill in the yard. The Auld Holland Inn is complete with windmill and the Kasteel Franssen Restaurant.

The "Holland Happening" each spring is a major celebration of Dutch heritage, featuring tulip displays, Dutch dancers and dancing, an arts and crafts fair, Dutch foods, many special exhibits, activities and parades.

Lynden, Washington, a small-city Dutch settlement with close ties to Oak Harbor has Holland motif store fronts, exhibits and signs in Dutch.

In Skagit County, Washington, are some of the largest tulip fields and growers in the world. Thousands of people from all over the country drive, bicycle or bus through the colorful fields each spring during the valley's two week festival.

Southwest
Texas

Nederland, Texas

Founded just before the turn of the century by immigrants from Holland, Nederland, "lowland in Dutch," played an important role in the rice and dairy farming of the area, but growth began in earnest with the discovery of the Spindletop Oil Field. The Windmill Museum, with twenty-five-foot revolving blades, has three floors of display of artifacts and exhibits that chronicle Nederland's Dutch heritage. The museum is located in Tex Ritter Park, named for the famed country, western singer.

Places Named Holland

There are many towns named Holland in the U.S. They can be found in the states of Arkansas, Georgia, Illinois, Indiana, Iowa, Kansas, Kentucky, Massachusetts, Michigan, Minnesota, Missouri, New York, Ohio, Oregon, Pennsylvania, Texas, Vermont, Virginia, and Wisconsin. Hollands too small to make the maps are in Colorado, Nebraska, and New Jersey. Three states have a Hollandale: Minnesota, Mississippi, and Wisconsin. Hollanburg is in Ohio; Hollandsburg in Indiana; Hollandville in Delaware, and Holland Patent in New York. Then there are New Holland, North Carolina, New Holland, South Dakota, and South Holland, Illinois. Canada has Holland, Manitoba; Holland Center, Ontario; Holland Landing, Ontario; and Huallen, Alberta.

Golden Gate Park

The Old Dutch Mill, standing eighty-five feet high in San Francisco's Golden Gate Park, was built in 1902 for $25,000. It utilized the westerly Pacific breezes to pump 20,000 gallons of fresh water an hour to a reservoir 200 feet above ocean level. It was so successful that banker Samuel G. Murphy gave $20,000 in 1905 to build the Murphy Windmill, standing ninety-five feet high and pumping 40,000 gallons an hour. In 1913, motorized pumps were installed. Over decades, the mills became neglected and vandalized; sails were removed and the entrances sealed.

A group formed in 1964 by Eleanor Rossi Crabtree, daughter of the late Mayor Angelo J. Rossi, eventually raised $117,000 toward restoration. Total cost, including government funds, was $224,000. This effort restored the Dutch Mill, but the Murphy Mill has suffered major deterioration, and efforts are still underway to obtain funds for its restoration, especially since it is located next to the Queen Wilhelmina Tulip Garden.

Though the mills no longer operate, they are still popular tourist attractions and stand as solitary sentinels welcoming ships to San Francisco.

The Friesen Mill

The Friesen Dutch Mill located in Heritage Park, Hillsboro, Kansas, represents a continuity with the past and a sustenance of the present. The original settlers in this area of South Central Kansas represent Anabaptist/Mennonites who were forced to leave the Netherlands and move to Prussia during the era of the Reformation. As promised freedoms began to erode in 1874, many emigrated to the New World. Included in this group of some six thousand

Illustration by Diane Heusinkveld

was the Jacob Friesen family, who built the first Dutch-style mill in the Gnadenau Village, near present Hillsboro. In 1994 the descendants of the Jacob "Miller" Friesen family funded the construction of a working replica of the mill in its current location.

For the Mennonites, the Dutch windmill was a symbol of their migration story from the Netherlands — to Prussia, to Russia, to America — and a reminder of their long-since homeland in Holland. It was also an integral tool of sustenance, for as long as the mill was running, all was well; there would be food for the family and feed for the livestock.

Each May, the city of Hillsboro celebrates it cultural and ethnic heritage with a full day of activity including: food, music, house and farm crafts, and other special events. Though many of the activities represent German and Russian heritage, the logo "A Touch of Dutch" has been adopted to emphasize the Dutch connection and the construction of the Friesen Mill replica.

— *Courtesy of the Hillsboro Historical Society and Museum*
Hillsboro, Kansas

William Penn
and Pennsylvania Dutch

William Penn, 1664-1718, was the son of an English father and a Dutch mother. After his expulsion from Christ Church College, Oxford, England, he joined the Quakers. He was imprisoned briefly three times — once for his religious views, once in the Tower of London for his writings, and once for his debts.

Charles II gave Penn land in America in payment of a Crown debt to his father, Admiral Sir William Penn, for whom the colony of Pennsylvania was named. The son granted the colony freedom of religion; founded Philadelphia as the "city of brotherly love;" welcomed Quakers and other victims of religious persecution, and established friendly relations with the Indians.

In the 1680s, he sold 5,000 acres to a group of Dutch Quakers. Known as "Pennsylvania Dutch," the group is really of German ancestry, although many passed through the Netherlands on their way to the New World. The "Dutch" part of the name is derived from *Deutsch*, the Saxon and German word for "German." In the late 1600s, most of the residents of the community that became Germantown, Pennsylvania were Dutch. By 1700, however, Germans dominated the town.

Silver candlesticks marked Leeuwarden, 1782, Pieter Meeter, E. 1812-1813. Presented to President Reagan and Mrs. Reagan on the occasion of the state visit of Queen Beatrix and Prince Claus, April 19, 1982.
Official photograph, White House, Washington, D.C.

Bells Make the Hours Sing

The Singing Tower

The Dutch have a saying: "Good schools and good bells are two signs of a well-managed city." Tower clocks in the Low Countries play a short tune just before the hour, called a *voorslag* (forestroke) to call attention to the great bell's sounding. These timely solos have been part of town culture for centuries.

In Holland, where carillons originated and thrive, they are called *klokkenspel* (bell play). Because churches already had spires or towers, they were first to possess carillons. Town halls and universities have them also. A carillon started with a few bells — four to ten. With more prosperity, more bells were added. Some mechanically played carillons exist, but more popular are the ones played by a master carillonneur seated at a keyboard using both hands and feet. Many Dutch towns take great pride in their carillons, and sponsor festivals and competitions featuring all kinds of music from folk songs to classical.

The Bells of Victoria

Nearly ten tons of bells are in the famed Netherlands Carillon Tower, a famous landmark in Victoria, the capital city of British Columbia, Canada. Surrounded by a garden of flowers, the carillon is across the street from the majestic, vine-covered Empress Hotel in Victoria, and near the provincial government buildings.

Cast in Holland, these carillon bells from the west shore of the Old World, ring out from the west shore of the New. The journey of the bells was the path of migration of the Dutch-Canadians, who have become an important ethnic group in British Columbia. In gratitude for their New World home, they donated the carillon. Its cornerstone was laid in 1967 by Queen Juliana, mother of present Queen Beatrix. The carillon was dedicated in 1968, the year following Canada's centennial. Activated by a time clock, the bells "make the hours sing" as do the carillons in Holland.

On Canada Day, July 1, and on Christmas Day, the provincial

71

carillonneur plays special music. There are recitals also at three in the afternoon on Sundays, and from July 1 through September 15, the five octaves of bells can be heard in concert at noon on Wednesdays and at six in the evening on Fridays. Visitors, arriving at least twenty minutes before scheduled recital time, may be permitted to climb the stairs of the tower and observe the carillonneur.

Netherlands Centennial Carillon Tower, illustrated below, is in Victoria, British Columbia, Canada. Illustrated by Diane Heusinkveld.

Above: Klokkenspel (glockenspiel) *located at Pella, Iowa, one of few in the United States, is a memorial to the late H. Stuart Kuyper, former president of the Pella Window Company. It was dedicated during the fiftieth anniversary of the Pella Tulip Festival, May 1985.*

Famous and Familiar Names

U.S. Presidents

United States Presidents of Dutch descent include: James Madison, Martin Van Buren, Zachary Taylor, Ulysses S. Grant, Theodore Roosevelt, and Franklin D. Roosevelt. Also of Dutch descent was Jefferson Davis, president of the Confederacy.

President Martin Van Buren

Eleanor Roosevelt (1884-1962) could remember elderly relatives speaking Dutch occasionally in conversation. She was a niece of Theodore Roosevelt and fifth cousin, once removed, of her husband Franklin D. Roosevelt.

Both Roosevelt presidents and Eleanor were descendants of Claes Martenszen van Rosenvelt, who emigrated from the Netherlands to New Amsterdam in 1649. Theodore pronounced the surname to rhyme with "choose" or "roost." Franklin pronounced it to rhyme with "rose."

Former President George Bush, a descendant of the Pilgrim fathers, traces family ties to this God-fearing group of people who settled in Leiden in 1609 and left for America in 1660.

Familiar Names

Many Americans of Dutch descent have become widely known. One from earlier times was Cornelius Vanderbilt (1794-1877), who made a fortune in shipping, started the New York Central Railroad, and founded Vanderbilt University at Nashville, Tennessee. His Dutch parents were poor farmers on Staten Island, New York.

Known to millions are Dr. Benjamin Spock for his writings on baby and child care, and Walter Cronkite, a television newsman.

Names familiar to theater-goers include Cecil B. De Mille,

73

Humphrey Bogart, Henry Fonda, Jane Fonda, and Audrey Hepburn.

Writers include Walt Whitman, Herman Melville, Carl and Mark Van Doren, Pearl Sydenstricker Buck, Peter De Vries, and John Updike.

In sports, there are pitcher Johnny Vander Meer, and football coach Norman Van Brocklin.

Successful businessmen include Gilbert C. Van Camp in foods and John Manning Van Heusen in shirt manufacturing. In 1931, the late Peter Kiewit of Omaha founded a construction firm, Peter Kiewit Sons', Inc., which grew into a corporation with billions of dollars in revenue. The spectacular direct sales firm, Amway Corporation in Ada, Michigan, founded by Richard De Vos and Jay Van Andel, both of Dutch descent, in 1959 as a basement operation marketing household products, has revenues exceeding $1.1 billion annually. The nation's second-largest window manufacturer, Rolscreen Company of Pella, Iowa, was founded by Peter Kuyper.

James Van Allen, for whom the earth's radiation belts are named, is of Dutch ancestry. His rocket and satellite studies of cosmic rays and the aurora borealis led to the discovery of the vast belts of radiation which astronauts must avoid.

What's in a Name?

In translation, some Dutch surnames are perplexing. Among the puzzles are Blootebill (bare thigh), Lach (laugh), De Haan (the rooster), Kool (cabbage), and Nagel (fingernail).

In 1811, when Napoleon ordered the Dutch to choose surnames, some Netherlanders chose nonsense names, either out of spite or because they were certain that Napoleon would be overthrown and surnames would be dropped. Some of the hardy Dutch showed their contempt by choosing such names as *Naaktgeboren* (Born Naked), *Dodeman* (Deadman), *Grizel* (Horror), or *Hogenboezem* (High Bosom). As it turned out, Napoleon was overthrown, but the surnames stayed.

Some names stem from occupations. Two examples are: De Jager (the hunter) and Vander Molen (from the mill). Location gave birth to names such as Van Klompenburg (from the wooden shoe town) and Vander Woude (from the woods).

74

De Jong (the young) and Den Ouden (the oldest) initially indicated the family position. De Koning (the king) and Braafhart (brave heart) reveal family pride.

Among names best known in America are Van Buren (from the neighborhood), Stuyvesant (blowing sand), and Roosevelt (field of roses).

Dutch English

The word "Yankee" probably derived from the Dutch name Jan Kaas (John Cheese), a name the English used for Dutch buccaneers. Later, the New England Dutch applied the term to Connecticut traders whose business ethics were not to their liking. Eventually, "Yankee" came to refer to all Americans.

Dutch food words adopted into the English language include: *kool sla* (coleslaw), *koekje* (cookie), and *wafel* (waffle).

Examples of other Dutch words adopted into English are: *baas* (boss), *landschap* (landscape), *schaats* (skate), *snoepen* (snoop), and *jacht* (yacht).

The terms "Dutch treat," "Dutch uncle," and to be "in Dutch" originated with English-speaking people.

Historically Dutch

The Dutch influence is apparent in many East Coast place names.

The Bowery began as a road to Peter Stuyvesant's *bouwerij*, or farm. Wall Street was *de wal*, a set of palisades erected for protection against Indian raiders.

Brooklyn is a respelled version of the Dutch *Breukelen* (broken land). Harlem was *Nieuw Haarlem*, Gramercy was *De Kromme Zee*, and Flushing was *Vlissingen*.

Coney Island started out as *Konijn Eiland* (rabbit island). Rikers Island, a New York prison, was named in honor of a Dutchman named Reigers.

In the Hudson River Valley, town names such as Catskill, Plattekill, and Fishkill are derived from the Dutch *kil* (creek).

The Dutch language was widely used on the East Coast for more than a century after the English took over. It remained the language of the Dutch Reformed Church in the area until the 1800s.

A Strong Heritage

Dutch American Heritage Day

On November 16, 1776, four months after the United States declared its independence from Great Britain, a small brig of war, the "Andrew Doria," sailed into the harbor of the Dutch island of St. Eustatius in the Caribbean. Upon entering the bay, the governor of the island, Johannes de Graaf, ordered his forces to return the gun salute. This action made the Netherlands the first country to officially salute the flag of the newly-independent United States.

On November 14, 1991, the U.S. Congress and President George Bush proclaimed November 16, 1991, as Dutch-American Heritage Day. Through House Joint Resolution 177, Congress designated this day to recognize Dutch Americans who have played key roles in the economic, social and political life of the United States of America.

Dutch American Heritage Day is celebrated annually on November 16, throughout the United States, with ceremonies and special events.

The majority of Dutch Americans live in California, Florida, Illinois, Iowa, Michigan, New York, Ohio, Pennsylvania, Texas, and Washington.

Reformed Churches

Wherever one finds a cluster of Dutch people in the United States, a Reformed church is usually nearby. Half a million American Dutch are members of Reformed churches. Four denominations are part of the Dutch Reformed tradition: Reformed Church in America, Christian Reformed Church, Protestant Reformed Church, and Netherlands Reformed Church. Outsiders often have difficulty distinguishing between the denominations, but many of those within the Reformed churches consider their theological differences significant.

Six American colleges have close ties with Reformed churches. Associated with the Reformed Church in America are: Central College in Pella, Iowa; Hope College in Holland, Michigan; and

Northwestern College in Orange City, Iowa. Closely tied to the Christian Reformed Church are: Calvin College in Grand Rapids, Michigan; Dordt College in Sioux Center, Iowa; and Trinity Christian College in Palos Heights, Illinois. Enrollment at the six colleges is about 10,000. Five of the six colleges offer Dutch language courses.

Dutch Studies

A number of other major universities offer Dutch language programs and Dutch lectureships. They include Columbia, Harvard, Stanford, U.C.L.A., and the Universities of Georgia, Hawaii, Indiana, Maryland, Massachusetts, Michigan, Minnesota, North Carolina, Pennsylvania, and Texas.

The University of California at Berkeley offers a degree in Dutch studies.

Christian Schools International

Christian Schools International (C.S.I.) was founded in 1920 by members of the Christian Reformed Church, a denomination begun by Dutch Calvinists. Starting with thirty-seven schools, it has grown to 400 schools serving over 77,500 students. Headquarters are at Grand Rapids, Michigan.

Dutch-American Clubs

There are seventy-four Dutch-American organizations in twenty-four states and the District of Columbia. Twenty-one of these clubs are in California.

Oldest in California is the Netherlands American Society of Southern California. Its members meet monthly for Dutch food and fellowship. They celebrate the Queen's birthday with a dinner dance, and the freeing of the Leiden (city in Western Netherlands) with a feast of *hutspot* (stew) and herring.

In Redondo Beach, the Netherland Social Service Organization provides any assistance needed by recent Dutch immigrants.

In Anaheim, the 1,000 members of *Alle vermaak is ons* (A.V.I.O., all pleasure is ours) sponsor dances and parties.

Dutch club *Neerlandia* seeks to foster good relations between

Dutch and American citizens, and to promote understanding of the traditions of both countries. It sponsors monthly dances and charter flights to Europe, and issues a monthly magazine.

In Oakland, the East Bay Holland Club owns a clubhouse where members attend dinners, dances, and holiday parties.

Based in Grand Rapids, Michigan, the Dutch Immigrant Society (D.I.S.) publishes a quarterly magazine for its 7,200 families. "Coffee Hours" are arranged at various locations in western Michigan, where members get together for good conversation (in Dutch if they choose) and kinship. The D.I.S. also sponsors periodic worship services in Dutch.

The Netherlands-American Medical Society takes an interest in medical science in both countries and fosters the scientific and educational advancement of its members.

The Netherlands-American Academic Circle of New England meets four or five times each year to hear an invited speaker discuss some aspect of Dutch culture.

Founded in 1892 by twenty descendants of pre-1776 Dutch immigrants, the Netherlands Society of Philadelphia takes special interest in the Dutch history of the East Coast.

Membership in the Holland Society of New York is limited to descendants in the direct male line of pre-1675 Dutch residents of New York or the American colonies.

1656 Blue Laws

A 1656 New Netherland law prohibited the following activities on Sunday: "Any ordinary labor such as Ploughing, Sowing, Mowing, Building, Woodsawing, Smithing, Bleaching, Hunting, and Fishing." It also prohibited "frequenting Taverns or Tippling houses, Dancing, playing Ball, Cards, Tricktrack, Tennis, Cricket or Ninepins, going on pleasure parties in a Boat, Cart, or Wagon before, between or during Divine Services." In 1663, the following prohibitions were added: "roving in search of Nuts and Strawberries and…too unrestrained and excessive Playing, Shouting and Screaming of children in the Streets and Highways." [sic]

Growing Up Happy
in a Dutch Town

by Marvin R. Hiemstra

Each year the arrival of the new telephone book in Pella, Iowa, was eagerly awaited. After everyone was satisfied with the details of their own listings, the following painful realization would be whispered again and again in church, in the auto shop, and at the Tulip Time Costume Exchange: "Did you notice all the names in the new telephone book that *aren't* Dutch?"

Pella is somewhat unusual for an ethnic settlement, because the initial population was so large. Approximately 786 Dutch people appeared, in one moment, on a tract of prairie land in the middle of Iowa in 1847. Many of those who immigrated to Pella within the following decades were related to the original 786. With a few exceptions, it was a truly homogenous community and remained such through the 1960s, and still remains so in spirit.

If you brought a classmate home after school while in third grade, your mother would proudly announce, "X is your fourth cousin because...." Generally the connections were good.

Mistakes, however, were not forgotten — ever! "I don't want you running around with X because you know" — of course, you didn't and couldn't care less — "what X's great grandfather did on the Saturday night years ago after that band concert in July!"

If a Pella young person became amorously involved with a potential mate from a neighboring town or from a college other than Central the wail would rise, "Oh, why can't you marry a nice Dutch girl (or boy)? Do you want to break our hearts? Doesn't Pella mean anything to you?"

It was painfully apparent to most in their late teens and early twenties that their fellow Dutch girls and boys were not all necessarily nice mates. It was a bit of parental contradiction, since the young people had already been carefully briefed about which of their age group — and the parents attached — were *"hol in de Bolle"* (empty-headed and consequently acted somewhat crazily).

If a Pella-bred person brought a non-Pella-bred husband, or wife, into the community, this would never be forgotten. If twenty years later, two genuine Pella citizens strolled in front of a house and a serious crack was discovered in the sidewalk, one would invariably turn to the other and say, "You know, of course, the wife is *not* from Pella."

On a more positive note, I am delighted to report that there was a genuine concern about the destinies of young Pella products on the part of many adults in the community. Not all those who grew up in Pella could remain because of job limitations and special talents did appear that required special handling.

In my case, it was discovered quite early that Marvin had a definite way with words. What was he going to do about it? I remember with tears of joy a townsman, whom I scarcely knew, insisting that I come to see him. He had spent great time and effort investigating the University of Iowa Writers' Workshop. He presented the information to me and informed me that was my next step. I did attend the university, where I received an honors degree in creative writing and the beginning of my career.

In Pella, to describe something as really Dutch is the highest form of praise: "Her new boy is so cute....looks exactly like a Dutch baby." There is always, at least, a token interest in genuine Dutch culture. If a Pella man begins to move into middle-age and develops a somewhat picturesque appearance, someone will pipe up and announce, not necessarily to the satisfaction of the man in question, "He's beginning to look like a Frans Hals painting."

For some, the history of Dutch painters remains a mystery. When Pella's handsome Strawtown Inn named some of the rooms and suites after Dutch artists, confusion reigned concerning the Vermeer Room. Those, not familiar with that seventeenth-century artist's quiet, atmospheric, domestic scenes, engaged in spirited debate attempting to determine which of the Pella Vermeers the suite noted.

Pella's greatest gift to me is an understated humor that quietly strikes with delicious force. When one encounters a Pella person in the outside world, one immediately asks about Pella. "I hear they are going to install a real Dutch canal, but they haven't figured out how to keep the teens from sailing their cars into the water. Amsterdam has a special motor bureau that fishes cars out of the canals all day long."

A rare understanding of the limitations of prosperity and heritage promotion was delightfully stated in a Community Night skit. Someone marched onto the stage in Pella's rooster outfit — always a favorite at Tulip Time — and brought down the house with: "Hi there. I'm from Pella. Did you know that *all* our alleys are paved and, not only that, we have a lagoon shaped like a wooden shoe!"

One delightful Pella couple loved to walk in the evening, and if they sauntered by and discovered someone was not at home, the couple would go in quietly, turn all the chairs neatly upside down and leave. It was their signature. The smiling, not-at-home, folks would call the next day, apologize for not being in, and invite the "chair flippers" over for coffee that evening. We believed this was a clever idea invented by the couple, but years later, Dutch friends in the Hague informed me that this game has always been played by Dutch people who wanted to give their friends a chuckle.

Tulip Time was much awaited each year, especially by the young — first grade through high school. It was a joyful, bustling time at the most beautiful season, the first part of May. A young person might march in the band; help construct or ride on a float; perform Dutch folk dances; help with the special meal preparations and transportation services needed for the tidal wave of visitors, and have a great time. My fourth grade appearance as a beaming child on "The Old Woman Who Lived in a Wooden Shoe" float was captured on a postcard and distributed for years.

The usual schedules for almost everyone disappear, so Tulip Time really becomes a traditional European festival of hosting and merrymaking. Pella people of all ages work together to produce the incredible achievement of three days jammed with unique Dutch heritage activities enjoyed by immense crowds. The quality of cooperation and planning necessary is amazing and a wonderful learning experience for all involved.

Working very hard in agriculture and industry in the brisk climate of a wind-swept prairie, it is understandable that the successful Pella Dutch quickly developed a culture where food was of great importance. The town's economic structure blossomed with a combination of Dutch persistence and God-given good fortune. The abundance of food became a much-loved symbol of that success. Despite energetic attempts of the quasi-medical advertising world to suggest that everyone, whatever the age, should look like a seventeen-year-old gymnastic champion, the Pella Dutch happily continue to munch blissfully. A five-meal day is the tradition.

Breakfast is definitely not continental, but might include eggs, bacon or ham, toast, cottage fries, hot cereal, milk, fruit, and, of course, coffee. The same type of sturdy breakfast meal is enjoyed in the Netherlands today.

Morning *koffie tijd*, coffee time, or *kopje koffie*, a little cup of coffee, is a social event in Pella: at a friend's, neighbor's, or relative's house, or at a cafe with a business associate. In the country, the farmer will come to the house, or the farmer's wife may bring coffee time out to the field. The "meal" is never just a *kopje koffie* in the Pella area because the coffee is served with an avalanche of sugar and a third of a cup of cream, a sandwich of dried beef on a currant bun, *Krakelingen* (crisp figure-eight cookies), Dutch Letters, and whatever pastry looked good in one of Pella's bakeries that morning.

Lunch is a full-blown meal, not an elegant snack as it often is in Holland. There is *Erwtensoep* (pea soup), or Dutch potato salad or both, a main course — favorites are *Vleesballen* (spiced meatballs with gravy), *Runderlappen* (braised steak), and *Vleescroquetjes* (meat croquettes) — Dutch Crust bread, and a baked dessert à la mode, and coffee or iced tea served with the ubiquitous avalanche of sugar.

Afternoon *kopje koffie* or *koffie tijd* is more substantial than its morning twin since the evening meal may not come until seven, or later if work is being done in the fields. This "snack" is intended to assuage the stress of the day and provide fuel for the remaining hours of activity. The sandwiches are cold-cut paradise: perhaps slices of Pella bologna and Dutch cheese with caraway seeds. *Saucijze Broodjes* (pigs-in-a-blanket), are afternoon favorites. By this time, someone has whipped up a mile-high cake, or *Kletskopjes* (lace cookies), or *Appeltaart* (Dutch apple pie) just out of the oven, topped with fresh whipped cream sprinkled with cinnamon.

Dinner is a very serious meal. There are no words to express the complexities and the subtleties of the delicious menus served at Pella tables. People frequently eat themselves silly. Groans and shrieks of "Oh, I ate too much!" echo around the town. Fortunately, since walking and biking are now in fashion, people do exercise for awhile. Thank God for two golf courses and a beautiful walking path to Red Rock Lake.

82

Dutch Determination
A Family Story

by Harriet Heusinkveld

Dick Heusinkveld and wife Ella De Boer Heusinkveld, of Sioux County in Iowa, were both first generation Americans. Their children have continued in cultural patterns determined by Dutch ancestry — membership in the Dutch Reformed Church and throughout the generations, attending Reformed Church colleges. A determination to succeed in the New World was a notable family value.

Newly married, Dick's parents, Hendrikus and Hendrika Heusinkveld, left Vaarseveld, Gelderland, the Netherlands, and sailed for America in 1881. He was twenty-seven; she was twenty-five. Determined to find a wonderful new life, they left the farm on which they were hired servants and fled the prospect of being drafted into the military. After traveling rough seas for seventeen days, they reached the "promised land." Soon they were speeding westward by train to Greenleafton, Minnesota, where Uncle Evert Heusinkveld had preceded them in the American experience. While living with Uncle Evert, Hendrikus attended rural school for a year in order to learn the English language — an early determination of the value the family would place on education.

The spell of the West gripped Hendrikus and Hendrika, and they moved on to homestead 160 acres in the Dakota Territory — land of their own! But it proved to be a harsh land; even the winter blizzards and destructive prairie fires, were overshadowed by the hot, dry winds and summer droughts which destroyed their promising wheat crops almost every year. They were "dirt" poor with a family of five children. All had to work the farm, especially Dick as the eldest, who did the work of a man while yet a boy. He chafed under this routine, since he had a keen desire for learning, however, he managed to get some school books and studied them diligently after the farm work was done. When he was about fifteen, he finally had the chance to attend the Springfield Normal School (high school), where even though he had spent only a couple of years in grade school, he tested into the 10th grade. He graduated on to the Sioux Falls Business School, after which he went into a law office in Armour, the Douglas County seat. There he "read law," hoping to become a lawyer some day. Soon he received a position in the bank of Hull, Iowa. It was in Hull that he met and married our mother, Ella De Boer.

Mother's father, Gossen De Boer, came to America at age seventeen with his widower father from Terschelling, one of the Dutch Frisian Islands. In 1882, he met and married Mintje De Roos, who had come to America in 1873 at the age of eighteen with an extended family group of sixteen from Oosterlittens, Friesland, the Netherlands, where her father had been a dairy products wholesaler. They settled on a farm near Orange City, Iowa. Their first year in America coincided with a grasshopper plague that lasted five years, so they were never as prosperous as they had been in the Netherlands.

After their marriage, Gossen and Mintje moved to Hull. Here they had five children, and were quite successful in acquiring land in the area, eventually owning eight farms of 160 acres each. Since her father was relatively well-off, Ella, our mother, second to the youngest, enjoyed privileges not usually afforded girls by the old Dutch attitude. She finished high school and went on to Hope College in Holland, Michigan. She was also an accomplished pianist. While teaching at a rural school near Hull, she met and married our father, who left his job at the bank to take over one of the De Boer farms in 1915.

Six children came into the family — myself (Harriet), George, Henry, Myron, Willis, and Frances. But tragedy struck in December of 1929 when Mother died. At thirteen and in the 10th grade at the time, I was the eldest; Frances, the youngest, was only three. Relatives and others advised that I should quit school to help care for the other children, but Father, whose own obsession for learning had been thwarted, was adamant that his children be educated despite all the difficulties. To insure this wish, he immediately took out a $1,000 policy for each of us, just in case he should die early. The amount was a large sum at the time.

Hired girls and hired men came and went, and we all worked hard to keep the farm and house going. Some relatives and neighbors were critical that we children did not stay at home as full-time help, but to realize a Dutch father's obstinate dream of having all his children educated, we worked harder. It was a great sacrifice on the part of our father.

Even though he was blind toward the end of his life, he typed the story of growing up in South Dakota so we would remember the strength of our heritage. He died in 1970, but was satisfied during his lifetime that all of his children attended Northwestern Junior College in Orange City; four finished at Central College in Pella and two at Iowa State University, Ames. Myron, Frances, and I received Ph.D. degrees; George a Master's degree, and Henry and Willis, Electrical Engineering degrees.

In a way, this reflects the fulfillment of the dream of Hendrikus and Hendrika, who left positions as land servants in the Netherlands to seek a more complete life. Today, they would find that their heirs, the children of Dick and Ella, have contributed to and enjoyed their dream. I, the eldest, enjoyed a career of teaching at Central College in Pella, Iowa; George worked as a reporter on the Oskaloosa Daily Herald until his death in 1981; Henry worked as an electrical engineer for aircraft companies in California; Willis was the systems engineer for Iowa Southern Utilities in Centerville, Iowa, and Frances was a professor of music at Buena Vista College in Storm Lake, Iowa.

In the 90s, all are enjoying retirement, but still lead full and busy lives through hobbies and activities. You may find Henry leading hiking groups in California; Myron singing with the Valley Choral Society in Livermore, California; Willis enjoying leisure-time as an avid bird-watcher; Frances still playing the organ in her own and other churches, and I researching books on local history and geography.

To carry on the legacy, all eleven grandchildren have received degrees of significant academic achievement as professionals in their fields. There are sixteen great-grandchildren; the four oldest, as of this writing, are in first and second years of college; the others follow with the youngest in first grade.

I am reminded of a line from Shakespeare's *Merchant of Venice:* "How far a little candle throws his beams!" Likewise, the fulfillment of our parents' dreams cast a light on the lives of their children throughout the generations.

Affirmation of Heritage

by Margaret Wolffensperger-Kleis

In 1947, I was at home in Zwolle, Overijsel, the Netherlands, where I grew up in a household with a large family, and where intellectual pursuits were a matter-of-fact. This tone was, in a large measure, set by our mother who was the first female student at the Technical University in Delft at the turn of the century. So when I was offered a scholarship by Hope College in Holland, Michigan, upon graduation from high school in Zwolle, it was considered a great opportunity for me to "spread my wings" through study abroad. We had learned much about the United States after World War II, and this was also the year of the Centennial of the City of Holland.

Upon accepting the scholarship, I had exactly nine days to get ready. We left the harbor of Rotterdam on the S.S. Tabinta with 1300 people on board, mostly immigrants bound for Canada. But as soon as I boarded, I was introduced to twenty-two other students; fifteen were going to Holland, Michigan. The nine-day boat trip was adventurous fun for us as single teenagers, but for the immigrants who did not know if or when they would see their families again, it was an emotional trauma with many tears shed.

The S.S. Tabinta originally was a freighter used for troop transport during the war and was now chartered for immigrants. One deck was for women and children; another for men and older boys. The bunks were triple high, so I chose a top bunk of little use to young children or to mothers who had to get up from rest frequently. Often, I helped the mothers look after little ones, since I had learned to help others in my work at home. Our household, for a period of three years during the war, included five elderly aunts, a Jewish family, and two young children, which gave us all great opportunity for caring and never a dull moment.

After docking in Montreal, we traveled by train to Kalamazoo, Michigan, where we were met by Hope College staff and driven to the campus. Here we met our roommates and were assigned lodging for the year. It did not take us long to get used to things; the professors were very helpful, speaking a bit slower to give us a chance to catch on. Names like Dijkstra, Kleinheksel, Pieters and

VanderPloeg were familiar to us. The older people we met, proud of their Dutch heritage, were eager to practice the Dutch language in helping us. Other students were very receptive, inviting us to different events and asking us about our country and customs — no, we did not wear wooden shoes, except during the war when leather was at a premium. Many invited us to their homes for vacations. After two months in the U.S.A., I considered myself an American student, having spoken English in my sleep.

Since I needed spending money, I took a job, working three hours each afternoon, at the H.J. Heinz Company. Having no car required walking the two miles to and from my work; I would get a ride once in a while. My work was in a very quiet department, where we put small pickles in a special design into small jars. This gave me a chance to talk with other workers from whom I learned almost as much as I did in the classroom. This was my first close contact with factory workers; they told me about their families, their interests, their foods, and they invited me to their homes.

Having adjusted well and not being homesick, I chose to continue my studies at Hope. I was granted a scholarship for another year, though for a lesser amount, but I could work during the summer months to earn money for room and board. During the first summer, I stayed with a doctor's family, where I learned to entertain and to cook; at the same time, I held down a job as chambermaid at a local resort. It was an opportunity to meet many different people.

After three years, I graduated and married Ken Kleis, an American of Dutch descent, and for the next few years, I worked at a five-and-dime and a department store. This allowed me to interact with Mexican and other Spanish-speaking people, mostly migrant workers, since I was the only clerk who spoke their language.

At that time, there were more Dutch-speaking immigrants coming to Holland, and I was able to help them, especially the women, with their English. Men working outside the home could pick up language skills at their jobs, but women were usually homebound with little opportunity to learn English. Many of the women were homesick and lonely, and being able to talk to them in Dutch, as well, helped them adjust. Yet, I knew of one family that returned to the Netherlands because the mother was so homesick. Fortunately, I was able to go home for visits and my family came to Holland frequently.

The strength of close family ties has endured over the miles and years. During World War II, families had to bond together and extend that bond to others in need for survival. My parents taught lessons of a lifetime by their example. My father was a civil engineer who refused to work for the German occupation forces; my mother was a Christian who firmly believed in the basic human principle, "Do unto others as you would have them do unto you."

We had a large house, ten bedrooms, and since my brothers and sisters were away much of the time, the space became a safe place for the underground. Our regular household members averaged around seventeen during the war years. Among them were my father's aunt, ninety-five years old, and her two single daughters; his two older sisters, both in their seventies. They were homeless after the Germans confiscated the homes of retirees. We also were sheltering, literally hiding, a Jewish couple and a little Jewish boy and girl. My older brother, who was a medical student, would bring American pilots who had been shot down and had found their way to the underground. We had a good hiding place under the dining room floor with short term provisions, which we had to use only four times, but we practiced securing it regularly.

To deter the Germans from entering our home, at one time a sign, appearing quite legal, was placed on our front door. Written in German, it read:

> IMPORTANT NOTICE
> A CHILD DIAGNOSED WITH DIPHTHERIA IS
> LIVING HERE. ENTER AT YOUR OWN RISK.
> Signed: Dr. E. Engelhart

Two times, we actually saw German patrols coming up our walk, but they turned back upon reading the notice. There may have been others.

During my junior year in high school, after D-Day in 1944, schools were confiscated so we were home all day. One of my jobs was to cut firewood for the two pot-bellied stoves and the kitchen range, and to keep them fired — there was not enough fuel for our central heating system. Breakfast was served in shifts; rooms had to be cleaned; we ground the wheat for pancakes and cooked sugar beets for syrup. Our ration coupons did not provide for our real household, so we often had to pick up, illegally, extra milk at night.

We made frequent trips to the store to redeem our ration coupons. The young Jewish boy, who was five at the time, would go with us until one time, I was approached by someone who remarked that he looked Jewish. I quickly replied that he was our cousin, and we quickly rode our bicycles home. He was then moved to the country. We learned, later, that he was captured and sent to a concentration camp, but he survived. The girl lived with us from 1941 until the end of the war.

Jewish family members were usually separated when hidden so they would not be picked up all together; this allowed a better chance that someone would be left to carry on the family.

At night, the Jewish couple, my sisters and I would play games, and sometimes, after dark, go for a walk. Routinely at nine o'clock p.m., we tuned in the short wave of Radio Nederland, which gave updates on the allied forces on the war front. A map marked with daily progress was posted on the wall.

My training and these experiences at home in the Netherlands, coupled with my experiences in Holland, Michigan, have given me a deep appreciation for the people and the American way of life, especially in the Midwest, but I will never forget my Dutch heritage. For my three children and nine grandchildren, America is their homeland; all are proud of their heritage, but they appreciate the Dutch memorabilia and treasure the customs as well. America is my country too! And I hope that I have made a contribution of some measure by being actively involved in community and church, both socially and politically. *Oost West, Thuis Best!* — East West, Home is Best!

Memories of
South Holland, Illinois

by Marilyn Newmeyer

My family moved from Chicago, south to the suburb of South Holland, Illinois, in 1954. I was six years old, but the smell of cabbages, and the feeling of being surrounded by tidy "fragrant" farms, lingers. Onion sets and cabbages seemed to be the crops of choice. I recall a neighbor who diligently swept her own driveway, and then extended her efforts down the street. Windows gleaming, showing Dutch lace or white curtains were predictable, but charming nevertheless.

The pattern of life seemed predictable also. I attended Calvin Christian School, named after the Protestant Reformation leader, John Calvin. Many of us had names beginning with "Van." My parents, Ernest Van Hattem, now deceased, and Hazel (nee Hoving), were born in the United States, both of Dutch descent. Church and school activities were a main focus in our family, as members, first, of Bethany Christian Reformed Church, and later, charter members of Cottage Grove Christian Reformed Church. As a child, I received a thorough indoctrination in the Bible and the tenets of the Christian Reformed Church. In the course of my professional training at the Presbyterian St. Luke's School of Nursing in Chicago, I first realized not everyone was tall with blonde hair. I was the second tallest girl in my class!

Even though I have been settled in California for twenty-six years, far from South Holland, and married, "out of the fold," to Fred, my wonderful German husband, early childhood memories linger like the warm aroma of sweet treats — *Banket, Jan Hagels* — and on New Year's Day — *Oliekoeken* — coming from our kitchen. And the pattern continues with the recent marriage of our son Joe to Kathie, a beautiful Dutch girl, who once resided in South Holland and attended Calvin Christian School.

Journey to a Dutch Village

by Dorothy Neil, Honorary Hollander

In 1925, when our family moved from the Scandinavian-settled Skagit Valley in Washington to Whidbey Island, we found that Oak Harbor, Washington was a "Dutch village."

The town had been settled in the early 1850s by a predominantly Irish contingent, including sea captains and disappointed Gold Rush miners from California. There was free land. One boat came from Australia with three Irish families, whose descendants still live in Oak Harbor.

When the Dutch immigrants began to arrive in 1894, there was much land to be developed. They cleared the forests, plowed the land and planted, raised their families, built schools and churches, started businesses, and served in government. Today, after over a hundred years on Whidbey Island, they have contributed much to making Oak Harbor and Island County a desirable place to live.

In 1941, the Whidbey Island Naval Air Station — to become Ault Field — came to North Whidbey and took over Clover Valley where many of the early Dutch immigrants had made their homes since pioneer days. The farmers moved across the Deception Pass to Skagit County, where they now raise tulips. The fertile fields of Skagit produce world-class tulips, and are a popular tourist spot in April. One gardener wrote to the Netherlands for genuine Dutch tulip bulbs; they wrote back saying they hadn't received their shipment of bulbs from Skagit Valley as yet, but would send them as soon as they arrived!

In Oak Harbor, the Dutch went into business — bakeries, bicycles, groceries, and others. During the years, mayors by the name of Eerkes, Van Syke, Zylstra, and Koetje have served. Mayor Al Koetje served twenty-four years.

Each April, the town celebrates "Holland Happening" with a parade, a Dutch food buffet at the First Reformed Church, arts and crafts, wooden shoe making, Dutch dancing, street sweeping, and other special traditional activities. The ethnic diversity of Oak Harbor has expanded due to the Navy, but they are all "Dutch" on Holland Happening Day. The parade is led by the mayor, who also leads the Irish Parade on St. Patrick's Day! Brilliant displays of tulips and a variety of spring blossoms make this one of the Northwest's prettiest festivals.

A large windmill at City Beach welcomes boaters to Oak Harbor's marina. Holland Gardens, surrounding a windmill, is ablaze with color each year. Entering Oak Harbor from the north, one is greeted by yet another large windmill at the Auld Holland Inn and Kasteel Franssen Restaurant.

My work on *The Dutch Book,* celebrating one-hundred years on Whidbey Island from 1894 to 1994, took me on a journey into the past and present of early Dutch settlers and their descendants. The book tells the story of the Hollanders, the "verhaaltjes"— little stories, pictures, and family histories.

Their contributions abound: John Vanderzicht, whose father was Oak Harbor's first marshal, was Washington state's Director of Parks. Today, Barney Beekma, whose grandfather settled Clover Valley and built one of the first schools, is a Representative to the State Legislature. Oak Harbor will always be a "Dutch Town!"

One of the series of tiles designed by Dorothy Neil
that help finance Oak Harbor's Holland Happening.

Dutch Discipline

by Dennis Visser

Growing up on a farm in Sioux County in northwest Iowa, reverently referred to as the Dutch ghetto, secured memories and an ethic of work and discipline which I value more and more with time. My origin, and that of a large majority of the population there, is the small European country, the Netherlands.

A central part of our family life was the church. The Reformed denomination, with the influence of John Calvin, directed the values I received from the Christian Reformed Church. That influence surrounded the community, the home and school.

I was baptized by a pastor who received some degree of notoriety when *Life* magazine featured him as a "Hell, Fire and Brimstone" preacher. Notable among his efforts was the success of keeping a movie theater from opening in Sioux Center, Iowa. Thus, growing up was free of the outside influence of movies — that is, until you reached driving age and the "maturity" to go to another town to sneak in a show without parental permission. The movies we "sneaked" would be rated a "G" by today's standards. Dancing and card playing were other entertainments strictly forbidden by this conservative influence.

Elementary school was a small local Christian school run by the parents of about sixty children, all with similar family backgrounds. Religion was integrated into most classes, continuing into a consolidated Christian high school. Excellence and discipline in academics, sports, and other activities were expected. Our entertainment centered around school and church group events. A strong sense of community through fund-raisers, suppers, and work projects intertwined the ethnic and religious ties. The annual Tulip Festival was a celebration we looked forward to, but I recall being more interested in the carnival and rides than the ethnic dances, street washings, plays, and Dutch costumes.

Family meals were always together, with rare exceptions during the harvest season. These were preceded by prayer and closed with Bible devotions, usually led by our father. On Sundays, after church, the extended family, including aunts, uncles, and cousins, would convene at our grandparents' home for a meal. While the

Elizabeta and Teunis Visser, grandparents, were born in Kralingen, Netherlands in the 1880s and came to Sioux Center, Iowa.

adults visited, we played in the far reaches of the basement, or ran around the town's neighborhood. This was a welcome change from the isolation of the farm during the week.

Being one of four children in a farm family, meant many activities were dictated by the farm season. There was many a prayer for rain or sunshine, and thanksgiving for answered prayer. It was okay for farm boys to be excused from school when help was needed beyond the regular daily chores of milking and cleaning the hog house. The exhilaration of the completed harvest and a job well done is a vivid memory. There are the smells of the fresh-cut silage and the foods that would feed the neighbors, uncles, and cousins, who provided the extra manpower when needed. These were hands-on lessons in the strength of cooperation and loyalty.

But this feeling of security did not expand the experience of interacting with different cultures. Leaving the "Dutch ghetto" to attend the "big" University of Iowa in Iowa City, challenged that gap. This mind-expanding plunge proved, in its way, to be as exhilarating as harvest time. I believe the healthy outcome centered on values secured growing up in a Dutch-American family and community in rural northwest Iowa. I am grateful!

Passing on the Heritage

by Carol Van Klompenburg

As a squealing and laughing toddler, I bounced on my grandfather's knee to the rhythm of a Dutch nursery rhyme. Although I didn't understand the meanings, I mimicked his rolling and guttural sounds, sing-songing them after him. The language of my ancestors, sifted through four generations, was still sprinkled in my life.

Grandpa Addink always started his joke in English and, without realizing it, slipped into Dutch on the punch line.

When my father said, "Well, *vrouw* (wife)," after an evening of visiting, he meant, "Time to go home." And when my mother called me a *bengel*, I had been naughty.

When Grandma Kiel felt *benauwd*, it was hard for her to breathe, and when a house was *gezellig*, it was warm and cozy. "Ach," my grandmother would say, "there just aren't English words for some of those things. Some of my twenty uncles and aunts would nod agreement, supplying other examples of untranslatable words. Eventually, my fifty cousins and I began nodding our heads and agreeing, too.

Not just words, but whole sayings were woven into my life. A long thread — a lazy seamstress," said my mother when my long thread became tangled. I had tried to hem a skirt without having to rethread the needle. Then she said it in Dutch, remembering, "My Grandma Huisman always said that."

Whenever I thread a needle — using a short thread — I'm sure my great-grandmother would approve. She'd probably say, *De appel valt niet ver van de boom*." (The apple doesn't fall far from the tree.)

Religious life was important to us. Before each meal, as his father and grandfather had done, my father recited the Lord's Prayer. And, as did the generations before, my siblings and I recited, "Lord, bless this food, for Jesus' sake. Amen."

When clan members addressed our church pastor as *dominee*, they demonstrated both affection and high esteem. Church life, complete with two full-length Sunday services and weekday meetings, was an important part of our heritage.

My father remembers the era of a third service in Dutch each Sunday. But now the services are in English, and the occasional singing of a Dutch Psalm — part of my childhood memories — becomes less frequent, as the number of Dutch language singers declines.

Families, often large ones, were a valued part of my life. Derogatory statements about relatives were forbidden.

Orderly life was important, too. Every good housewife had her Sunday dinner prepared by Saturday evening, her wash on the line early each Monday morning, and her spring cleaning done before Easter.

Hearty Dutch dishes like *erwtensoep* (pea soup) and *hutspot* (Dutch stew) were my favorites. I thought the whole country ate *banket* (almond pastry) and *Sinterklaas koekjes* (Santa Claus cookies).

Today I realize with regret that everyone hasn't bounced in rhythm to a Dutch nursery rhyme or tasted *hutspot* and *banket*.

However, when I forget to put salt in the *oliebollen* (Dutch doughnuts), I warn my family they will taste *flauw* (flat). Before a meal I sometimes say to our sons, *"Eet smakelijk!"* (Eat heartily!)

I use the Dutch proverbs in English. When I realize that our sons are eavesdropping, I remind Marlo, "Remember, little pitchers have big ears." My grandmother said, *"Kleine potjes hebben grote oren."* When my oldest son accuses his brother of being stubborn, I tell him that the pot is calling the kettle black. My mother said, *"De pot verwijt de ketel dat hij zwart ziet."*

Although our three sons pray spontaneously instead of reciting the table graces of my childhood, we still begin and end our meals as our ancestors did. The beliefs of our forbears are our faith, too.

In our family, the heritage changes and grows — as we pass it on.

Nailhead painting is a folk art that originated in the Dutch village of Staphorst. Individual nailheads, or circular clusters of them on a spool-like holder, are dippled in paint and then applied to wooden objects or clothing. The example shown here is a crafted round box with lid.

Holiday Traditions

by Carol Van Klompenburg

Family birthdays are important events in the Netherlands, often celebrated at an all-day open house. A birthday calendar is traditionally posted as a reminder of the birthdays of immediate family members as well as those of aunts, uncles, cousins, nieces, nephews, and acquaintances.

Following a church service, New Year's Eve, like most holidays in the Netherlands, is spent at home. Families play games and eat a light, cold supper, with drinks at midnight. Traditional fare includes a herring or salmon salad, Dutch doughnuts and apple fritters.

At Easter, the children play a special game called *eiertikken,* — bumping eggs together and seeing whose can remain unbroken the longest. In the eastern and southern provinces, Easter bonfires are lit to celebrate the arrival of spring.

Sinterklaas
(St. Nicholas)

Sinterklaas has been a part of Dutch folk tradition for centuries. Each December 5, clad in red velvet robes and carrying a bishop's mitre, *Sinterklaas* arrives in Amsterdam by boat and rides his white horse through the city streets.

St. Nicholas was a fourth-century Christian bishop in Asia Minor. In the eleventh century a church was built at Bari, Italy, as a shrine for his bones, and his popularity grew rapidly. He became the patron saint of Russia, and of children, sailors, and prisoners. In the Netherlands, twenty-three churches were dedicated to his memory in the twelfth and thirteenth centuries. The joyous celebration of St. Nicholas Eve, December 5, and St. Nicholas Day followed.

Dutch settlers brought the tradition to America. Dutch children learned that *"Sint Nicklaas"* rode over the rooftops on a white horse, bringing goodies for children and was accompanied by a lit-

Peter. Colonists with other language backgrounds adopted the tradition, resulting in "Santa Claus" for St. Nicholas.

The switch from December 5 to Christmas Eve is noted in Clement C. Moore's 1883 poem, *A Visit from St. Nicholas*. In 1863, Thomas Nast illustrated the poem, giving Santa Claus the appearance we know today.

In the Netherlands and among many Dutch Americans, the *Sinterklaas* celebration continues to be in early December. In California, the Dutch club *Neerlandia* sponsors a *Sinterklaas* dance, with an appearance by the saint. *Sinterklaas* parties are sponsored by the Netherlands American Association of Minnesota, the New Orleans Holland Club, the East Bay Holland Club of Oakland, California, and others. In Holland, Michigan, the Dutch Village has a year-around display with life-size replicas of *Sinterklaas* and his Black Peter assistants. In Pella, Iowa, *Sinterklaas* leads a parade accompanied by his *Zwarte Piet* (Black Peter) helpers, who help him distribute gifts to the children at Scholte Church.

Children in the Netherlands, at bed time, leave a snack on the table for *Sinterklaas*. And near the fireplace, they put a pair of

wooden shoes containing a bit of hay for his horse. When they awaken the next morning, *Sinterklaas* has eaten the snack, taken the hay for his horse, and left each child a present — perhaps a piece of fruit or a toy. When older children find a piece of coal instead of a gift, it means they are now too old for *Sinterklaas*.

Adult gift-giving is also timed for *Sinterklaas* Day. The Dutch celebrate December 25 much as Americans celebrate Thanksgiving — as a happy, religious, family holiday. They attend Christmas services, read the Nativity story, sing carols and feast.

Sinterklaas

Illustration by Diane Heusinkveld

A Heritage of Rhyme

One simple Dutch nursery rhyme gives me as much pleasure as a Shakespearian sonnet. Why? Because it's the rhyme of my grandfather. He sat me on his knees and bounced me to its rhythm. My mother did too. Now she bounces my children to the same lilting sounds. And so do I.

In family tradition, a child knows that the exciting part of the ride will come with the repeated nonsense words *"Kafoeps! Kafaps!"* In any language those words can mimic the sounds of a galloping horse. The words are repeated as often as adult and child wish. —*Carol Van Klompenburg*

Kafoeps! Kafaps!

Hee! Hee! Paardje op een draf.
Morgan is het Zondag.
Dan komen de heren
Met de mooie kleren.
Dan komen de vrouwen
Met de wijde mouwen.
Dan komt Jan de akkerman
Met zijn paardje achteraan.

Kafoeps! Kafaps!
Kafoeps! Kafaps!

Hey! Hey! The horse is on a
    trot.
Tomorrow it is Sunday.
Here come the gentlemen
With their nice clothes.
Then come the ladies
With their wide sleeves.
Then comes John the farmer
On his horse at the rear.

Kafoeps! Kafaps!
Kafoeps! Kafaps!

From: *Dutch Nursery Rhymes*. Compiled by Elisabeth Kempkes, illustrated by Wilma Hadley. First printed in Dutch, 1939. Printed in English, 1979. *Weekblad*, Pella, Iowa.

99

Sinterklaas die goeie heer,
Die komt alle jaren weer.
Met zijn paardje voor zijn wagen,
Zoo komt Sinterklaas aanjagen.

Sinterklaas, good gentleman,
Visits every year again.
Wagon right behind his horse,
He speeds along his snowy course.

Klein klein kleutertje,
Wat doe je in mijn hof?
Je plukt er al mijn bloempjes af!
En je maakt het veel te grof
Och, mijn lief Mamaatje,
Zeg het niet aan Papaatje.
Ik zal zoet naar school toe gaan
En de bloempjes laten staan.

Little one, little one.
What are you doing in my bower?
Why, you're picking all my
flowers!
The pretty colors now are gone.
Oh, dear Mother,
Don't tell Father.
To school I will sweetly go
And leave the flowers to bloom
and grow.

Heb je wel gehoord van die holle
  bolle wagen
Waar die schrokkige Gijs op zat
Die kon schrokken grote brokken
Een koe en een kalf,
Een dood paard half,
Een os en een stier,
En elf tonnen bier,
Een kerk vol schapen.
En nog kon Gijs van honger niet
  slapen.

The wagon can only creak and
  shake
On it sits the glutton Jake
He eats a cow and a calf,
A horse and a half,
An ox and a steer,
Eleven tons of beer,
And a church full of sheep.
And hunger still keeps him from
  sleep.

Er was eens een vrouw	A wife once baked
Die koek bakken zou.	Her spouse a cake.
De pan viel om	The milk was sour
De koek was krom.	And costly the flour.
De melk was zuur,	The pan fell splat,
Het meel was duur.	The cake went flat.
De man kwam thuis	He gave a shout
En jaagde ze uit 't huis.	And chased her out.

Tweebeen zat op driebeen.	Two legs sat on three legs.
Toen kwam vierbeen	Then came four legs
Die wou tweebeen bijten.	Who bit two legs.
Toen nam tweebeen driebeen	Two legs picked up three legs
Om er vierbeen mee te smijten.	To smite four legs.

Who are they?
A man, a stool, and a dog.

Dutch Memory Verse

Harold Roelofs of Pella, Iowa, learned this verse from his grand-mother, who died when he was four. The twelfth verse of a Dutch Psalm, it was frequently memorized by Dutch children.

Opent uwen mond,
Eischt van mij vrijmoedig.
Op mijn trouw verbond;
Al wat u ontbreekt,
Schenk ik zoo gij't smeekt,
Mild en overloedig.

Open your mouth, repent,
Ask freely, knowing
That by my covenant
All that you lack to live
I'll very freely give
With love o'erflowing.

Counting in Rhyme

Ten little lemon drops in a long
    line,
One rolled away, and then there
    were _____.
Nine little lemon drops, but in
    came Auntie Kate;
She took the very biggest one;
    then there were _____.
Eight little lemon drops; along
    came greedy Marie,
She quickly picked up five of
    them;
Then there were _____.

Three lonely lemon drops. But at
    the corner store,
The clerk gave me an extra one;
    Then there were _____.

Four lovely lemon drops. In came
    my Uncle Ben;
He gave me six all for myself!
    Then there were _____.

Ten little lemon drops. I ate them,
    every one.
Now the fun is over. Now I have
    none.

The Nice Fat Lady

A nice fat lady in St. Paul
Baked cookies every day.
She baked and baked, pan after pan,
And gave them all away.
Her relatives, her visitors,
The children on her street
All thought her cookies were so
  good
They'd eat and eat and eat.
But when they said, "Now that's
  enough;
We've eaten all we can,"
She wouldn't stop because she still
Had batter in her pan.

The friends who came to visit her
Went staggering down the street;
Her cat looked like a cannon ball—
He had so much to eat.
Her dog and all her neighbor's dogs
Got bigger, rounder, fatter,
But yet she said she couldn't stop
Because she still had batter!

The teacher from the school next
  door
Brought all his pupils out
To see why people looked so
  round—
What made them groan and shout,
But when they saw the cookies there,
They all began to eat,
And soon they went a-groaning and
A-moaning down the street.

And when the neighbors shouted,
  "Stop!
This is a serious matter!"
The lady said, "I cannot stop
Because I still have batter."

The people from the factories—
Their bosses, too, it seems—
Fell down in rows along the walk,
All bursting at the seams.

Although the people got so fat
That they began to roll,
She wouldn't stop because she still
Had batter in her bowl.

But finally the people said,
"We can't eat anymore."
So then she piled the cookies up
In baskets on the floor.
She filled the houses and the barns,
And in the city square
She piled up the cookies till they
  made
A mountain in the air!
Alas! The mountain fell apart—
It made a noise like thunder;
And as it fell, the lady was
Completely buried under!
Just as she disappeared and heard
The cookie-thunder roll,
She said, "Oh, dear, and I still had
Some batter in my bowl."

There's still one thing I have to say
Before this story ends:
If you decide that you will bake
Some cookies for your friends,
Just think this over carefully—
It's an important matter:
It's dangerous to make too much
Delicious cookie batter.

Reprinted with permission of the publisher.

Annie Schmidt

Dutch writer Annie Schmidt has written twelve volumes of children's poetry. Forty of these poems were translated into English by Henrietta Ten Marmsel, Professor of English at Calvin College in Grand Rapids, Michigan, to create *Pink Lemonade*, published by Wm. B. Eerdmans Publishing Company.

Deliciously Dutch

We may live without poetry, music and art,
We may live without conscience, and live without heart,
We may live without friends,
We may live without books,
But civilized man cannot live without cooks.

— From: *The Pella Cookbook 1905*

In the cool Holland climate, Dutchmen enjoy a wholesome diet with an abundance of breads, vegetables and dairy products. Hearty stews, tasty breads and rich pastries are the essence of Dutch cuisine. Soups use a rich variety of Netherlands vegetables. Breads are laden with cheese, meats or chocolate shot. Rusks, which are crisp, dry buns, are sometimes substituted for bread.

A traditional breakfast may include a sandwich of white or brown bread with cheese, jam, chocolate shot or cold meat. Children may eat porridge *(pap)*. A boiled egg indicates a special occasion. Tea, milk and buttermilk are popular.

For Dutch city folk, lunch may also feature a sandwich — bread, rolls or rusks with liver sausage, ham, cheese, roast beef, tongue or smoked sausage. Often there are currant buns, cut thick and spread with butter, and a fresh fruit dessert. For guests, a soup, macaroni dish or croquette may be added. In restaurants, a favorite lunch is the "chucker out" *(uitsmijter)*, bread topped with thin-sliced beef or ham, and fried eggs.

In the cities the Dutch have their only hot meal of the day in the evening. It begins with a vegetable soup, followed by meat, potatoes and several vegetables. A typical dessert might be custard, stewed fruit, pancakes or apple tarts.

Rural Dutch eat their hot meal at noon and their second sandwich meal in the evening. Both rural and city folk punctuate their day with midmorning and midafternoon cups of coffee *(kopje koffie)* and snacks.

Apples and almond paste are favorite dessert fillings. For delectable Dutch letters *(banketstaven)*, almond filling is wrapped in a flaky butter pastry. Pigs in a blanket *(saiucijz-broodjes)* treat the palate to a spicy, meat-filled pastry.

Whatever the food, the Dutch make it easy to heed their pre-meal ritual comment, *"Eet smakelijk"*, a saying that defies translation, but means "tasty eating" plus, perhaps, "enjoy!"

105

Appetizers and Beverages

Advokaat

Mina Baker-Roelofs, Pella, Iowa, says Advokaat *is a Dutch "ladies' drink".*

2 eggs
1/3 cup sugar

1 cup brandy or apricot
brandy

Beat eggs until thick. Add sugar and brandy. Serve in demitasse cups or small glasses. Eat with demitasse or special Advokaat spoons.

Note: Mina says *Advokaat* will keep for 1 to 2 days in the refrigerator.

Farmer's Daughter Cocktail
Boerenmeisjes

Lois Boonstra Vogel of Orange City, Iowa, says that because of her preoccupation with her favorite hobby, her grandchildren call her the "golf grandma." Her husband, Frank, is president of Orange City's Diamond Vogel Paint Company.

At Christmas, while Dutch men are enjoying their boerenjongens, *the ladies traditionally sip* boerenmeisjes, *a sweeter drink.* Boerenmeisjes *is also often served to celebrate the birth of a baby.*

12 oz. dried apricots,
   finely chopped
2 cups warm water

juice of 1 lemon
2 cups sugar
2 cups apricot brandy

Soak chopped apricots in warm water for 8 hours. Add lemon juice and bring to a boil. Simmer for 20 minutes. Remove from heat and, while still warm, add sugar. Stir until sugar is dissolved. Add apricot brandy. Pour into jars, seal tightly and let sit for 6 weeks. Makes 2 quarts.

Serve in wineglasses with a tiny spoon for eating the apricot pieces.

Farmer's Son Cocktail
Boerenjongens

Helen Van Wesep De Vos of Grand Rapids, Michigan, is the daughter of Dutch immigrants of the late 1800s. She says, "I am a housewife who enjoys needlepoint, tennis and music. I have served on the board of the Grand Rapids Symphony and as chairman of the local Toys-for-Tots program. My proudest achievement, however, is our four wonderful children — the eldest of whom has recently presented us with our first grandchild."

Her husband Richard's grandfather emigrated from the Hook of Holland and came to America at the age of twelve, then saved enough money to send for the only family he had left, two brothers.

A traditional Christmas drink, boerenjongens, *is best if allowed to mellow for several months. Plan ahead if you'd like to serve it in the holiday season! In this recipe, wine is used instead of bourbon or brandy.*

1 1/4 cups sugar	1 cinnamon stick
1 cup water	3 1/2 cups sweet white wine
1 lb. golden raisins	1/2 cup vodka

Place sugar and water in a saucepan and heat, stirring until sugar dissolves. Wash raisins in hot water and drain. Add raisins and cinnamon stick to sugar water. Cook over very low heat until raisins are plump. Remove raisins with a slotted spoon and place in large-mouth bottle with an airtight lid. Boil the liquid down for a few minutes until slightly thickened. Remove cinnamon stick and pour the syrup over the raisins. Cool thoroughly. Add wine and vodka. Seal and bottle. Let the drink mellow at least 3 months before serving.

Serve in small wineglasses and eat the raisins with a small spoon.

Spiced Milk
Slemp

Carol Van Klompenburg, Pella, Iowa. Slemp *is the traditional drink for children at* Sinterklaas *parties.*

4 cups milk
6 cloves
1 cinnamon stick or 1/4 tsp.
   ground cinnamon

pinch of saffron
pinch of mace
1/4 to 1/2 cup sugar
1 teabag or 1 tsp. tea (optional)

Bring milk to a boil in heavy saucepan. Tie spices in cheesecloth. Drop into milk. Simmer for 1/2 hour. Add the sugar. Remove cheesecloth with spices, squeezing excess liquid into milk. Serve immediately with optional tea bag. Serves 4.

Anise Milk
Anijsmelk

Carol Van Klompenburg, Pella, Iowa. In the Netherlands, hot anijsmelk *is especially popular after ice-skating on a chilly winter night.*

1 qt. milk
1 Tbsp. sugar

1 tsp. anise seed, crushed

Heat milk just to boiling point. Stir in sugar and anise seed. Serve either hot or cold. Makes 4 servings.
Variation: To make Sage Milk (*saliemelk*), substitute 1 teaspoon powdered sage for anise.

Milk Tea

Eunice Robijn De Soto, Tacoma, Washington, was given this recipe by her Dutch grandmother.

4 cups milk
1 Tbsp. black tea

sugar to taste

Heat milk almost to boiling. Add tea and sugar. Steep 15 minutes. Strain and serve hot.

Savory Balls
Bitterballen

Strawtown Inn of Pella, Iowa, serves bitterballen *as part of its special seven-course Dutch Dinner each November. Strawtown Inn features formal dining, European decor and such Dutch touches as Hindeloopen folk art and wooden shoe candleholders.*

Bitterballen are a favorite special-occasion appetizer in the Netherlands. They are not bitter, but are traditionally eaten at the "bitter hour" — after a workday — accompanied by a glass of Dutch gin.

2 Tbsp. butter
3 Tbsp. flour
1 cup chicken broth
1/2 lb. cold cooked veal,
    finely chopped
1 Tbsp. finely chopped parsley
1 tsp. nutmeg

1 tsp. Worcestershire sauce
1/8 tsp. freshly ground
    black pepper
2 egg whites
1/2 cup fine dry bread
    crumbs
oil for deep fat frying
prepared mustard, Dijon type

Heat butter in saucepan. Add flour and cook for 2 minutes, stirring constantly. Gradually add broth, stirring constantly, until a thick paste is formed. Add veal, parsley, nutmeg, Worcestershire sauce and pepper. Combine thoroughly. Refrigerate mixture for 2 hours. Heat oil for deep frying. Form meat mixture into 1-inch balls. Beat egg whites until foamy. Dip balls in egg whites, then roll in bread crumbs. Fry in oil for 2 minutes or until golden. Serve with hot mustard for dipping. Makes 35-40 balls.

Cheese Truffles
Kaastruffels
The Holland Cheese Exporters' Association

1/2 cup butter
1 cup shredded Edam or
    Gouda cheese
1/8 tsp. paprika

firm pumpernickel bread,
    crumbled into fine crumbs
parsley, finely minced

Cream butter. Combine butter, shredded cheese and paprika. Shape into small balls. Roll half in pumpernickel crumbs, half in finely minced parsley. Chill. Makes 24 truffles.

Holland Cheese Shrimp Bites

Holland Cheese Exporters' Association

2 cups shredded Edam or
    Gouda cheese
3 Tbsp. flour
1 tsp. baking powder
1 Tbsp. minced onion

1/2 tsp. dillweed
2 eggs, beaten
1/2 cup shrimp, cooked and
    chopped
oil for deep frying

Mix shredded cheese, flour, baking powder, onion and dillweed. Add beaten eggs and mix until cheese is evenly distributed in batter. Stir in shrimp. In a deep skillet or saucepan, heat oil to 375°F. Carefully drop teaspoonfuls of batter into oil. Cook until fritters are golden brown, about 3 minutes, turning once during the cooking period. Drain on paper towels. Serve hot. Makes about 3 dozen.

Dutch Fried Cheese
Gebraden Hollandse Kaas

"Sounds odd, tastes delicious...that's Dutch Fried Cheese," comments the Holland Cheese Exporters' Association, which recommends this recipe. The Association suggests serving fried cheese with beer.

2 egg whites
2 Tbsp. water
8 slices Edam or Gouda
    cheese, 1/3-inch thick

fine dry bread crumbs or
    cracker crumbs
butter or margarine

Beat egg whites slightly with water. Dip cheese slices into egg whites and then into crumbs. Let stand 10 minutes. Then sauté in butter or margarine in a skillet until golden brown on both sides. Makes 8 slices.

Pigs-in-a-Blanket
Saucijzebroodjes

Mina Baker-Roelofs, Pella, Iowa, says that Pigs-in-a-Blanket are a traditional pastry for Dutch coffee time, mid-morning or mid-afternoon.

Dough:

2 cups flour	1/2 cup shortening
1/2 tsp. salt	1 egg, beaten
2 tsp. baking powder	1/2 cup milk

Filling:

1 lb. lean pork sausage	2 Tbsp. cream
1/2 lb. hamburger	salt and pepper
2 Dutch rusks, crushed, or	
1/4 cup dry bread crumbs	

Dough: Sift dry ingredients together. Cut shortening into flour mixture. Mix beaten egg with milk. Mixture should total 3/4 cup liquid. Add to first mixture. Blend and knead 8-10 times on floured board. Divide dough into 2 parts. Roll each half of dough to a thickness of 1/4-inch. Make 15 rounds of dough from each half using medium-sized cookie cutter.

Filling: Blend filling ingredients. Form 30 small rolls, shaped like link sausages. Place on pastry round and seal edges.

Place filled pastries on a baking sheet with raised edges and bake at 350°F. for 40 minutes. Serve hot.

Note: Mina says Pigs-in-a-Blanket can be refrigerated or frozen after baking, and reheated for serving.

Tiny Dutch Pancakes

Poffertjes, tiny Dutch pancakes, are a traditional delicacy sold from *poffertjes kramen* (booths) in Dutch villages and towns in the Netherlands. Often they are sold from a colorful tent which is pitched at the village for a few days and moves on to market its tasty wares elsewhere.

Soups and Salads
Soep en Sla

Vegetable Soup With Meatballs
Soep met Vleesballetjes

Ria Outhuyse of El Toro, California, enjoys cooking Dutch. "Soups, stews, and mashed food (stamppot) *— ja, that is delightfully Dutch," she says. For three years Ria has written a column, "Ria's Hoekje," about health, cooking and beauty, that appears in a monthly newsletter. She confesses, though, that a quarter century of living in the United States has Americanized her family, too. "A steak on the grill, that is my husband's favorite!"*

1/2 lb. stewing beef	1/4 cup uncooked rice
8 cups water	2 small bay leaves
2 beef bouillon cubes	1 tsp. parsley flakes
4 stalks celery, diced	3/4 lb. ground beef
4 carrots, diced	1/4 cup bread crumbs
2 onions, minced	1 tsp. salt
1/2 cup small cauliflower flowerets	1/2 tsp. pepper
	1/4 tsp. nutmeg
2 tomatoes, peeled and diced	

Cook stewing beef in bouillon-flavored water until tender. Remove beef from water and add vegetables, rice, bay leaves and parsley flakes. Simmer until vegetables are tender. Mix ground beef, bread crumbs, salt, pepper and nutmeg. Form into small meatballs. Cut-up stewing beef and add, with meatballs, to soup. Simmer until meatballs are done. Add salt and pepper to taste. Serves 8.

Variation: Instead of adding salt and pepper to taste, you can season the soup with a soy sauce known as *maggi*. Ria says, "You will find *maggi* on every Dutch table in the Netherlands."

Pea Soup
Erwtensoep

For Margret Bloemendaal Rutgers of Lynden, Washington, erwtensoep was traditionally served as Sunday dinner in her childhood home in Iowa. She says, "It was prepared on Saturday, then slowly reheated on the back of our old wood stove on Sunday forenoon. We feasted on it after Sunday morning church services."

8 cups water	3 stalks celery, diced
2 cups split peas	4 leeks, diced
2 lbs. ham hocks	1 large onion, sliced
4 to 6 potatoes, diced	1 tsp. thyme
1 12-oz. pkg. smoked sausage	1 tsp. salt
links, sliced	1/2 tsp. pepper

Soak peas in water overnight. Add ham hocks and simmer, covered, for 2 hours. Remove hocks from pot, slice meat from bones, cut in small pieces and return to pot. Add potatoes, smoked sausage, vegetables and seasonings. Simmer 2 hours, or until vegetables are tender. Serves 10-12.

Oxtail Soup

Mina Baker-Roelofs, Pella, Iowa, has made eleven trips to the Netherlands, researching Dutch culture and foods.

1 oxtail, cut at joints	2 medium carrots, cubed
(or 1/2 lb. beef roast, sliced)	1 1/2 onions, coarsely chopped
1/2 tsp. salt	1 potato, peeled and cubed
1/4 tsp. pepper	2 stalks celery, cut fine
1 bay leaf	5 slices bacon, cut fine
1/4 tsp. thyme	1 Tbsp. sherry
8 to 9 cups water	1 to 2 Tbsp. chopped parsley
4 Tbsp. rice or barley	

In soup kettle, place oxtail or beef, seasonings and water. Bring to a boil. Simmer 3 hours. Strain broth. Remove meat from bone, or cut up beef slices. Return meat to broth and add rice or barley. Cook 25 to 30 minutes. Add carrots, onions, potato, celery and bacon. Simmer 30 minutes more. Add sherry. Garnish with parsley. Serves 6.

Tomato Soup
Tomatensoep

Wilhelmina Prins-Koeller, the Press and Cultural Affairs Officer for the Netherlands Consulate General in Chicago, moved to the United States in 1961. She says: "I visit the Netherlands at least once a year to see my mother and brother and sister and their families. During these visits I also notice changes in food habits. Grocery stores or the specialty greengrocers (groenteboer) now sell many fruits and vegetables that were not generally available thirty years ago, such as avocado, zucchini, kiwi fruit, mangoes, and ingredients for the diverse ethnic cuisines. The Dutch/Indonesian/Chinese cuisine has been popular in the Netherlands for many years, of course."

Wilhelmina remembers with delight the soups in her mother's Netherlands kitchen. "On days that mother spent most of her time washing clothes (before the arrival of the washing machine), soup was an all-day project and was served for the evening meal with sandwiches. Tomato soup was a favorite in my mother's home and now my own family enjoys its hearty taste just as much."

4 qts. water, divided
2 lbs. beef neck bones or
   beef shank
2 bay leaves
1 large onion, diced
4 lbs. ripe tomatoes, quartered
4 oz. ground beef
(1) 6-oz. can tomato paste

1 1/2 cups diced celery
   and leaves
8 to 10 sprigs fresh parsley or
1 Tbsp. dried parsley
4 oz. vermicelli
salt
pepper

Simmer 2 quarts water, beef neck bones, bay leaves and onion. In separate pan, simmer 2 quarts of water and tomatoes for 30 minutes. Put tomatoes through a sieve. Add tomatoes and liquid to first pan. Simmer until beef on neck bones is tender. Remove meat from pan. Cut meat from bones, dice and return to pan. Salt and pepper ground beef to taste, then roll into 1/2-inch balls and add to soup. Add remaining ingredients and simmer for an additional 30 minutes. Add salt and pepper to taste.

Variation: Wilhelmina suggests the following method if you wish to save time in preparation: Eliminate tomato paste from the recipe, and substitute a 28-ounce can of tomato purée for fresh tomatoes. Put 4 quarts water, beef neck bones, bay leaves, onion, and tomato purée in large pot. Then proceed as in above recipe.

Potato Soup
Aardappelsoep

Esther Wessels of West Sayville, New York, is second-generation Dutch stock. Both she and her husband, Abram, were born and raised in West Sayville, as were their seven daughters. Like many West Sayville Dutch-Americans, their ancestors emigrated from the Dutch fishing village of Yerseke in Zeeland.

6 potatoes, cut into bite-sized pieces	1 Tbsp. parsley flakes
	5 cups water
2 leeks, cut into bite-sized pieces	1 Tbsp. salt (or to taste)
2 onions, chopped	pepper to taste
1 carrot, pared and sliced	1/3 cup butter or margarine
1 stalk celery, sliced	1 13-oz. can evaporated milk
4 chicken bouillon cubes	chives, chopped

Put all ingredients, except evaporated milk and chives, in pot and simmer 3 to 4 hours. Stir in evaporated milk during last hour. If desired, mash vegetables before serving. Sprinkle chopped chives on top. Serves 6.

Alternative method: Instead of simmering 3 to 4 hours, cook in slow cooker on low for 10 hours.

Soup Without a Bone

Mina Baker-Roelofs, Pella, Iowa, says that using tiny meatballs as a source of flavor for soup is a common Dutch practice. She has made eleven trips to the Netherlands, researching Dutch culture and foods.

3/4 lb. ground beef	1/2 cup uncooked rice
6 cups boiling water	vegetables (optional)
1 large onion	

Shape ground beef into firm balls the size of small eggs. Place them in a large kettle and pour boiling water over them. (Water must be boiling when added to prevent meat from breaking.) Simmer meat for 15 minutes. Add onion and rice. Continue cooking until rice is tender. Add vegetables (celery, carrots, potatoes, beans, peas, etc.), if desired, and cook until tender. Additional water may be added if a thinner soup is desired.

Green Bean Soup
Snijboontjesoep

Johanna and Fred Oldemulders are from Holland, Michigan, where Fred has worked as a maker of wooden shoes since 1923. He began making shoes in the Netherlands at the age of 15, learning the trade from his father. Wooden shoes from this factory are in great demand for Holland's Tulip Festival each May.

Johanna says, "We have our own garden and I make the bean soup a few times in the summer. In the old country, bean soup was the Sunday meal, with pudding for dessert."

2 lbs. beef steak, cubed	1/2 cup chopped parsley
1 1/2 lbs. pork steak, cubed	7 beef bouillon cubes
3 qts. water	3/4 cup barley
1 1/2 cups diced celery	9 to 10 cups fresh green beans,
1/2 cup diced leek or	French cut
green onion	

Bring beef and pork to boil and skim scum from surface of water. Add celery, leek, parsley, bouillon cubes and barley. Transfer ingredients to pressure cooker. Bring to boil with the lid on and let steam come out. Then pressure cook at 15 pounds of pressure for 30 minutes. Release pressure. Remove meat and add beans. Simmer until beans are done. Combine meat and mixture in a larger pot and simmer a few minutes. About 8 quarts. Freezes well.

Farmer's Cheese Soup
Boerenkaas Soep

Margie Kolean-Knol of Holland, Michigan, edited "A Bit of Old Holland," a collection of Dutch and American recipes. In making this dish Margie suggests using homemade bread, cut 1/2-inch thick.

4 tsp. butter	1/4 lb. celeriac, diced
1 cup chopped onions	1 qt. chicken stock
2 carrots, pared and diced	4 slices lean bacon
2 potatoes, pared and diced	4 slices white bread
1/2 lb. cauliflower flowerets	1/4 lb. Gouda cheese, sliced

In heavy pan, melt butter. Add vegetables and cook for about 5 minutes, stirring frequently. Add chicken stock. (continued)

Bring to a boil and simmer until vegetables are tender, but not too soft. Meanwhile, in a heavy skillet, fry bacon until slices are brown and crisp around the edges. Remove and drain on paper towels. Fry bread slices in bacon fat until crisp and brown on both sides. Drain bread on paper towels.

Preheat broiler. Pour soup into ovenproof tureen or casserole. Float bacon slices on soup. Cover the bacon by arranging fried bread on top. Add sliced Gouda cheese to mask entire surface of soup. Broil 2 to 3 minutes until cheese melts and turns a delicate brown. Serves 4.

Meatball Soup
Balletjessoep

Marian Schoolland of Grand Rapids, Michigan, serves this soup as a main dish. Born in 1902, Marian is the author of some 20 books for children and for adults. Two of her books —"The Story of Van Raalte" and "De Kolonie" — deal with the history of the Christian Reformed Church, a denomination with strong Dutch ties. Marian also sends this advice: "Enjoy the good things God gave us, the beauties of nature and the great variety of good things to eat." Marian comments, "This soup tastes better the second day, as many soups do."

10 cups water	1 1/4 tsp. salt
salt to taste	1 egg
1/2 cup rice	1/2 cup white flour
1 lb. ground beef	2 or 3 carrots, pared
1/4 cup ground pork	2 stalks celery
1/4 cup wheat germ, cracker crumbs, or bread crumbs	1 large onion
1/2 tsp. nutmeg	1/2 cup vermicelli or very fine spaghetti (optional)

Bring water to boil, adding salt to taste. Add rice. Boil 20 minutes. Mix beef and pork with a fork, adding wheat germ, nutmeg and salt. Beat egg in a cup with a fork. Add to the meat mixture. Flour your hands and form meat mixture into balls slightly smaller than ping-pong balls. Flour the balls lightly.

Cut vegetables into small pieces. Add vegetables and meatballs to the boiling rice. Boil 20 minutes longer. Add vermicelli, if desired, to cook, uncovered, the last 7 minutes. Makes 8-10 servings.

Herring

Herring, sometimes called "the poor man's oyster" is to Dutchmen what the hot dog is to Americans. In season, it is sold at carnivals, fairs and food stands on city streets. No plates, knives or forks are required. A true Dutchman simply dips the raw, cleaned herring in chopped onions, lifts it by the tail, throws his head back, and munches upward.

Herring Salad
Haringsla

A former resident of Rotterdam, Cornelia (Nella) Breugem Kennedy is archivist and instructor in Dutch at Northwestern College in Orange City, Iowa. She comments, "Cold salads, such as herring salad, are very popular in the Netherlands and are generally served in cafeterias. In my family it was customary to have a cold supper at midnight on New Year's Eve, and we often had herring salad."

1 head lettuce
2 to 3 cups mashed potatoes
2 Tbsp. vinegar
2 Tbsp. oil
1/4 tsp. pepper
8 oz. pickled herring, drained
   and cut into small pieces
3 apples, diced
3 hard-cooked eggs, chopped

1/4 cup chopped sweet-and-
   sour pickles
1/2 medium-sized onion,
   chopped fine
8 oz. boiled beets, diced
2 Tbsp. cream, evaporated
   milk, or half-and-half
1 cup mayonnaise

Garnishes:
2 hard-cooked eggs, sliced
pickles paprika

parsley

Separate lettuce leaves. Clean and dry. Spread them on the serving dish. Mash potatoes with vinegar, oil and pepper. Add herring, apples, eggs, pickles and onion. Mix well. Add well-drained beets and stir carefully. Pack mixture on top of lettuce leaves in the shape of an igloo. Mix milk and mayonnaise and spread over mixture, covering it like an icing. Garnish with sliced eggs and any combination of pickles, parsley and paprika. Serves 8 to 10.

Nella says herring salad tastes best if made at least 10 hours before serving. She suggests, "If served as a dinner, serve fish soup first, then serve herring salad, accompanied by garlic bread or toast."

118

Dutch Lettuce
Sia in de Hollandse Stijl

Charlotte de Blecourt of Holland, Michigan, often fixes Dutch lettuce for her family of five. "My husband came to the United States from Garnwerd, a town in the Dutch province of Groningen," says Charlotte. "Our youngest son, Jahn, was born while we were visiting the Netherlands, so we have two Dutchmen in our family."

1 large head lettuce, torn in pieces	4 Tbsp. vinegar
	4 Tbsp. sugar
1 small onion, chopped fine	1 egg
5 or 6 slices bacon, diced	2 Tbsp. sour cream

Toss lettuce and onion together. Fry bacon crisp and remove bacon and drippings from pan. Combine vinegar, sugar and egg in bacon pan. Cook until thick. Stir in sour cream. Cool slightly and pour over lettuce and onion. Sprinkle with crumbled fried bacon.

Cooked Apples
Stoofappeltjes

Doris J. Vanden Berg and her husband, Laurens, run Vander Veen's Importing Company in Grand Rapids, Michigan. Doris says, "Dutch people love their Gouda cheese, chocolates, licorice, rusks, kale and rye bread, and we are here to supply them with these."

1/3 bushel (15 lbs.)Talman sweet apples	4 Tbsp. cinnamon
	9 cups water
5 cups sugar	1 1/2 Tbsp. cornstarch

Peel, core and quarter apples. Mix cinnamon and sugar together. Add to apples and water. Boil until done, about 20 to 30 minutes. Yields 8 to 10 quarts. Freeze in quart containers.

To serve, defrost 1 quart in medium saucepan. Bring to boil and add cornstarch that has been mixed with a little water. Serve hot with potatoes, gravy and meat.

Variation: Doris notes, "You can use Bosc pears instead of apples. Then the recipe is called *stoofpeertjes*."

119

Red Cabbage Salad
Poteten

Dutch Heritage Collection, Northwestern College, Orange City, Iowa.

1/2 lb. red cabbage	salt, pepper and mustard
2 apples	to taste
1/4 lb. bologna	1/4 to 1/2 cup mayonnaise

Shred cabbage fine. Core and dice apples. Cube bologna. Place ingredients in bowl and add salt, pepper and mustard to taste. Stir in mayonnaise. Serves 4.

Hussar Salad
(Dutch Potato Salad)
Huzarensia

Wilma Wesseling Schuringa emigrated from the Netherlands to Lansing, Illinois, in 1950. Wilma not only speaks Dutch and English, but she also teaches Spanish and German at Illiana Christian High School.

Wilma says, "Huzarensla is named after the hussars. When they invaded the Netherlands centuries ago, the dish they demanded most of all was the Dutch salad-meat dish, which was eventually named after them. It is still one of the most famous Dutch national dishes and is always served at parties."

6 medium-sized potatoes, boiled and cooled	6 oz. sour cocktail onions
	4 Tbsp. vinegar (or more)
3 medium-sized tart apples	4 Tbsp. mayonnaise (or more)
3 sour dill pickles	1/2 tsp. salt
1 1/2 cups cooled and diced roast beef	dash of pepper

Garnish:

2 hard-cooked eggs, sliced pickles, sliced	beets, cooked and sliced

Chop potatoes, apples and pickles into fine pieces. Add remaining ingredients. Mix well and pack into mold or bowl. Refrigerate for 3 hours. Unmold on a bed of lettuce. Garnish with eggs, pickles and beets. Serves 6.

Hot Potato Salad
Poteten

Elinor Noteboom of Orange City, Iowa, learned to make poteten (literally translated "pot eating") from her husband's maternal family. "Every spring he lets me know when the garden lettuce is ready, and we have poteten," says Elinor. "I have learned to enjoy this hearty, not-for-the-dieter dish."

Elinor is an artist, specializing in serigraphs. She writes, "Because of a tremendous need to release the vibrations going on inside my head, in the spring of 1976 I laid aside all teaching, sewing, and volunteerism. I put aside most socializing and some reading. Now I spend a steady six hours a day allowing this unknown quality to work its way from the area between my eyes —through my feelings — off my hands — and onto paper...a deep and quiet joy." Her "Festival Series," celebrating her Dutch roots, is based on Orange City's annual Tulip Festival.

Elinor suggests serving poteten with fresh sliced tomatoes or fruit salad. She adds, "Since it's not a colorful food, I like to serve it in a red or orange bowl."

5 average-sized potatoes	salt
1 lb. bacon, with drippings	pepper
1 qt. early leaf lettuce	6 hard-cooked eggs
1/2 cup cider vinegar	3 Tbsp. melted butter (optional)
onion salt	fresh parsley

Peel and boil potatoes until tender. Drain cool, slice and set aside in a large mixing bowl. Fry bacon and break into 1-inch pieces. Wash lettuce and pat dry. Add bacon and lettuce to potatoes. Pour on 1/3 cup vinegar and 1/4 cup bacon drippings. Mix thoroughly. Add onion salt, salt and pepper to taste. Chop 5 eggs and add to mixture. Continue adding more vinegar, bacon drippings (or butter) and onion salt until mixture looks like potato salad and tastes tangy. Lettuce will wilt, so to garnish use sixth egg and fresh parsley. Serves 6.

Dutch Potato Salad
Hollandse Aardappelsla

Deborah Haan of Sioux Center, Iowa, often serves this salad when spring lettuce first appears in her garden. Deborah hosts a daily radio show, "Family Room," in which she often shares her favorite recipes. Her husband Rev. B.J. Haan, is a pastor and a former president of Dordt College.

"We relish family gatherings, which usually center around food," says Deborah. "Entertaining dinner guests has been a big part of our life in the parsonage and in the president's home."

1 head lettuce or same amount of leaf lettuce	salt and pepper
4 large potatoes, boiled and cooled	8 hard-cooked eggs, sliced
2 to 3 Tbsp. butter or margarine	8 to 12 slices bacon, crisply fried

Vinegar dressing:

1/2 cup water	1/3 to 1/2 cup sugar
1/4 cup vinegar	1 Tbsp. bacon drippings

Shred or cut lettuce as for salad. Cut potatoes in small pieces and fry in butter or margarine. Add salt and pepper to taste.

For dressing, boil water, vinegar and sugar together until sugar is completely dissolved. Add hot bacon drippings. Pour mixture over lettuce. Layer lettuce, potatoes, sliced egg and crumbled bacon. Serves 6-8.

Pickled Beets

Built in 1874, the Cappon House Museum was the family residence of Isaac Cappon, the first mayor of Holland, Michigan. This beautiful Victorian home features original family furnishings and is open to the public. The following recipes for pickled beets and cucumbers are Cappon family recipes from the "old country."

Cook beets until tender. Skin and slice in bowl. Add sugar, pepper, spices, vinegar and water. Heat 1/2 cup each of water and vinegar with 2 Tbsp. sugar. A few pickling spices are added with pepper in a sauce pan. Let this boil a few minutes. Pour over beets and let stand until cool. This takes time. After cool and combined, let it stand for half a day or longer. Over night is better. Serve hot or cold.

Cucumbers

2 or 3 cucumbers depending on size	2 Tbsp. white sugar
salt	pepper
2 Tbsp. brown sugar	1/4 cup mild vinegar
	1/4 cup water

Peel and cut cucumbers crosswise into a glass or china bowl. Sprinkle generously with salt. Place a saucer or small plate (smaller than the top of bowl) to press on top of cucmbers. On top of saucer place a heavy can of food. Let stand 1 or 2 hours. Drain off juice. Sprinkle brown and white sugar over top of cucumbers. Add pepper to taste. Next add 1/4 cup mild vinegar and 1/4 cup of water. Cover and let stand in refrigerator over night. Serves 4.

Sauerkraut Salad
Sla van Zuurkool, Appels en Prei

Ria Outhuyse of El Toro, California, emigrated from the Netherlands in 1956. "After all these years of living in California," she says, "I still cook the Dutch way."

1 lb. sauerkraut	2 sprigs parsley
2 large tart apples	2 Tbsp. pimiento
1 leek	
Sauce:	
1 cup sugar	1/4 cup water
1/4 cup apple cider or wine vinegar	

Drain sauerkraut and cut fine. Dice apples. Mince leek and parsley sprigs. Mix sauerkraut, apples, leek, parsley sprigs and pimiento. Mix sugar, cider and water in saucepan. Heat until sugar dissolves. Pour sauce over vegetables; refrigerate overnight. Serves 4.

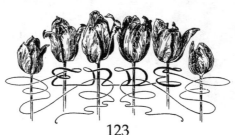

Fort Orange Baked Beans
Bonen in de Fort Orange Stijl

Evelyn Sturdevan of Albany, New York, is an avid gardener and has been a member of Albany's Tulip Festival committee for 33 years. She now chairs the judging for the county's outdoor planting contest.

Albany's early Dutch settlers used this recipe for baked beans when the city was still known as Fort Orange. Evelyn found this recipe in a settler's cookbook and has adapted it to modern cooking methods.

1 lb. dried navy or pea beans	1 cup maple syrup
2 tsp. dry mustard	1/4 lb. salt pork
1/4 tsp. coarsely ground black pepper	1 large onion, peeled and scored

Wash beans and soak overnight in enough cold water to cover. Bring to a boil and simmer for 1 hour. Drain, reserving water. Place beans in a 3-quart casserole. Combine mustard, pepper and syrup. Pour over beans, stirring constantly. Insert salt pork and onion into bean mixture. Add reserved liquid until it rises high enough to be visible in the beans, but does not cover them completely. Bake, covered, at 275°F. for 5 hours. Add additional reserved liquid if necessary. Uncover and bake for another hour or until tender. Serves 4.

Dutch Etiquette

According to a Dutch cook, currant bread is considered to be a special treat, and Dutch etiquette requires that a courteous guest eat only one piece.

Meats, Fish, and Main Dishes

Marinated Roast
Stoofvlees

Born in Amsterdam, Peter Spier grew up in Broek, a small village in the Netherlands made famous as the "birthplace" of Hans Brinker. Peter now lives in Shoreham, New York. He has written and illustrated more than 150 children's books. His "Noah's Ark" was the 1978 Caldecott Award winner. Peter is also the author and illustrator of the adult book "Of Dikes and Windmills".

1 2-lb. boneless chuck roast	3 peppercorns
1/2 bottle red wine	1/2 tsp. salt
2 onions, sliced	1/2 cup butter
1 bay leaf	2 Tbsp. flour
3 cloves	Worcestershire sauce
1 small carrot, sliced	salt

Marinate roast for 2 days before you plan to serve. To make marinade combine wine, onions, bay leaf, cloves, carrot, peppercorns, and salt. Turn roast in marinade several times a day. When ready to prepare, drain marinade and set aside. Dry the roast and fry in butter until golden brown. Sprinkle with flour and add half of marinade. Simmer, covered, for 1 hour. Stir and turn frequently. Remove lid. Continue simmering 1 1/2 hours, adding additional marinade as necessary. Remove meat from sauce and slice. Strain sauce, adding Worcestershire sauce and salt to taste. Serve with boiled potatoes and vegetables. Serves 4-6.

Meatballs
Vleesballen

Anne Heerema of Hollandale, Minnesota, uses this recipe for appetizers and for soups, as well as for an entrée. Anne grew up in northern Holland. She remembers, "Mother used a schedule for cooking: Monday erwtensoep, Tuesday stamppot. On Wednesday there was meat on the menu. Did that ever taste good! Lots of times it was meatballs. They really taste good with red cabbage."

1 lb. ground beef	1/8 tsp. allspice
1/2 lb. ground pork	1/8 tsp. cloves
3 Dutch rusks, crushed fine	1/4 tsp. pepper
1/2 cup milk	2 to 3 Tbsp. butter
1 egg	2 beef bouillon cubes
2 Tbsp. grated onion	2 cups hot water
1 tsp. salt	

Combine beef, pork, rusk crumbs, milk, egg, onion and spices. Shape teaspoons of meat into balls. Brown in butter. Dissolve bouillon cubes in hot water and pour over meatballs. Cover and simmer 30 minutes. Makes 5 to 6 servings.

If gravy is desired, stir 2 tablespoons flour into meat juices.

Holland Cheese
Chicken Rolls

Holland Cheese Exporters' Association

4 chicken breasts, skinned and boned	1/4 to 1/2 cup flour
	2 eggs, lightly beaten
8 wedges of Edam or Gouda cheese	fine bread crumbs
	oil for deep frying

Cut chicken breasts in half. Pound to about 1/4-inch thickness. Place wedges of Holland cheese on each half-breast, roll and tuck in edges so cheese is completely enclosed. Secure with skewer or toothpick. Coat with flour, then dip into beaten egg. Roll in bread crumbs, completely coating chicken roll. Allow chicken rolls to dry 10 to 15 minutes. Fry in hot oil at 325°F. until golden brown, about 10 minutes. Makes 4 servings.

Cheese Casserole

Netherlands-American Resource Center, Holland, Michigan

6 slices stale white bread
5 Tbsp. butter
6 thick slices Gouda or Edam
   cheese (about 10 ounces)

2 eggs
1 cup milk
salt and pepper to taste

Trim and butter bread slices. Arrange them slightly overlapping, in a buttered 1-quart casserole. Cover with cheese slices. Beat eggs with milk. Add salt and pepper. Pour over bread and cheese. Dot with 1 tablespoon butter. Bake 30 minutes at 350°F. until golden brown. Serve piping hot.
Suggestion: Serve with green salad.

Meat Dish
Hachee

Barbara Beerda De Haan lives in San Marcos, California, where the De Haans and their five children moved when they emigrated from the Netherlands in 1958. Barbara suggests serving this hearty winter dish with mashed or boiled potatoes.

1 lb. stewing beef
2 Tbsp. flour
1/2 cup butter or margarine
1 1/2 lbs. onions
1 bay leaf
1 clove

1/2 pkg. brown gravy mix
5 cups water
1 to 2 Tbsp. vinegar
salt, pepper and seasoned
   salt to taste
1 to 2 Tbsp. cornstarch
   (optional)

Cut the meat into small pieces and mix with flour. In large skillet heat the butter or margarine and fry the meat until brown. Slice the onions and add to the meat in skillet along with bay leaf and clove. When the onions are golden brown, add the gravy mix, mixed with a little water to make a paste. Add the remainder of the water. Cover pan and simmer for an hour. Add vinegar. Season with salt, pepper and seasoned salt. Remove bay leaf. If desired, thicken with cornstarch mixed with a little water to make a paste. Makes 4 or 5 servings.

Seasoned Steaks
Runderlapjes

The Netherlands-American Resource Center, Holland, Michigan

2 lbs. round steak, cut in 4 slices
salt
freshly ground pepper
1/2 cup butter, oil or bacon
    drippings
2 medium onions, sliced

2 Tbsp. wine vinegar
2 tsp. prepared mustard
1/2 cup water
1 bay leaf
cloves
peppercorns

Score the meat and rub with salt and pepper. In a large frying pan, using half the butter, brown meat thoroughly on both sides. In another frying pan, using the rest of the butter, fry onions over medium heat until transparent. Mix vinegar, mustard and water, add to onions and pour over meat, scraping to loosen any particles from bottom of skillet. Add seasonings. Cover and simmer 2 hours, or until very tender, turning every half-hour.

Serve meat on heated platter surrounded with boiled or mashed potatoes. If desired, strain sauce and thicken with a little flour. Pour sauce over meat. Red cabbage is a popular Dutch complement to this dish.

Cabbage-Hamburger Casserole

Marlene Blankespoor, Holland, Michigan, provided this hot dish for a Dutch meal with the Blankespoor clan on a Christmas Eve.

1 lb. lean ground beef
1 medium onion, diced
1 head cabbage, coarsely shredded

(1) 10 1/2-oz. can tomato soup
1 cup water

Sauté ground beef with onion until cooked, but not brown. Place shredded cabbage in a 2-quart casserole. Add beef and onion. Mix tomato soup and 3/4 cup of water. Pour over beef and onion. Bake at 350°F. for 1 1/2 to 2 hours, until cabbage is tender. About 8 servings..

Note: More water may be added if a thinner sauce is desired.
Suggestion: Serve over a bed or rice.

Sweet-Sour Cabbage

Margaret Kleis, Holland, Michigan, remembers this as a favorite during World War II when she was one of 15 to 18 people at the family table each day.

4 strips bacon	1/2 cup sugar
1/2 cup onion, chopped	1/2 cup vinegar
1 head cabbage, coarsely chopped	salt and pepper to taste

In a large frying pan fry bacon with onion until crisp. Remove bacon and some of drippings from pan. Chop bacon and return it to pan. Add cabbage, sugar and vinegar and bring to boil. Cover and simmer 1 1/2 hours on low heat, or until tender. Season with salt and pepper. Simmering 1/2 to 1 hour may be enough if people like crispier vegetables. Serves 4-6.

Note: 1/2 pound ground pork sausage may be used in place of bacon.

Suggestion: Serve with mashed potatoes and fruit. Margaret says, "During World War II, whenever possible, we served meals in one dish, so we mixed the mashed potatoes with the cabbage for easy serving. Leftovers were made into patties and fried the next day.

Vegetable-Sausage Stew

Launa Riepma, Oak Harbor, Washington, learned to prepare this main dish from her husband's family.

6 to 8 potatoes, peeled and quartered	1 ring Polish sausage
	water to cover
6 to 8 carrots, scraped and sliced	salt to taste
	butter

Place potatoes in bottom of large saucepan or Dutch oven. Add a layer of carrots. Place sausage atop carrots. Add water to almost cover vegetables, and salt to taste. Cover and simmer until vegetables are tender. Remove sausage and about half of the cooking liquid. Mash potatoes and carrots together, adding more cooking liquid if needed. Cut sausage into individual portions. Serve vegetables with pat of butter on each serving. Serves 6.

Note: Onions may be included in the vegetables if desired.

Pete's Stew
Pete's Hutspot

The late Peter H. Kuyper of Pella, Iowa, was the hutspot maker for his family. Pete used ground meat for his recipe, just as his mother had done when she prepared it each washday. The hutspot could simmer unattended while she did the family wash.

Pete was particular about his hutspot recipe. When he passed it on to his children, he included a diagram showing the proper way to layer the combination during cooking.

1 lb. ground round steak	2 lbs. carrots, sliced
1 lb. ground pork	1/4-inch thick
3 lbs. potatoes, peeled and	1 lb. onion, cut in eighths
sliced 1/4-inch thick	salt and pepper to taste

Sauté ground meats in large pot, stirring until lightly browned. Add vegetables and enough water just to cover vegetables. Cover tightly and cook until vegetables are tender. Mash lightly until well mixed. Season to taste and serve hot. Serves 8-10.

To eat *hutspot* in the Kuyper style, serve with applesauce and homemade bread. *Hutspot* freezes well and tastes especially good reheated in a microwave oven.

Scholte's Stew
Scholte's Hutspot

Dominie H.P. Scholte emigrated from the Netherlands and founded Pella, Iowa, in 1847. The Scholte house is open for tours during Pella's annual Tulip Time and year-round by appointment. This recipe for hutspot has been handed down through generations of the family.

6 carrots, pared and sliced	2 Tbsp. butter
6 onions, peeled and sliced	1 tsp. salt
10 potatoes, pared and quartered	1/4 tsp. pepper
1/4 to 1/2 cup milk	1/4 tsp. sugar

Boil carrots and onions until very tender. Drain. Boil potatoes separately. Drain thoroughly. Add carrots and onions to potatoes.

(continued)

Mash very fine. Add milk, butter, salt, pepper and sugar. Stir and reheat. *Hutspot* should have the consistency of mashed potatoes. *"Serve Scholte's hutspot with fried pork chops and gravy," advises Leonora Gaass Hettinga, great-granddaughter. "Sometimes I serve it with steak, too, but I really prefer pork."*

Blind Finches

Strawtown Inn of Pella, Iowa, offers formal dining in an Old World Atmosphere.

8 5-oz. portions veal,
   thinly sliced
1 lb. ground beef
1/2 tsp. salt
1/4 tsp. pepper
1 tsp. nutmeg
1 Tbsp. finely chopped onion

1 Tbsp. finely chopped parsley
4 eggs
2 rusks, crumbled fine
vegetable shortening
1 can (10 1/2 oz.) chicken
   or beef broth

Sauce:

1 Tbsp. onion, finely chopped
1/2 lb. mushrooms, sliced
3 Tbsp. butter
1 tsp. lemon juice

1/4 cup flour
1 cup chicken or beef stock
1/3 cup red wine
1/2 package dry oxtail soup
mix

Pound veal slices to 1/4-inch thickness. Mix well the ground beef, salt, pepper, nutmeg, onion, parsley, eggs and rusks. Divide into 8 portions. Roll a slice of veal around each portion and tie securely with string. Fry in small amount of shortening until well-browned. Drain and place in bottom of a roasting pan. Add the broth to pan in which veal rolls were browned, scraping well to loosen all particles of browned meat. Pour over veal rolls. Cover and bake at 325°F. for 1 1/2 hours, or until tender.

Sauce: Sauté onion and mushrooms in butter. Add lemon juice and simmer 2 to 3 minutes. Add flour to make a roux and add chicken or beef stock, wine and oxtail soup mix. Simmer, adding more wine, stock or boiling water until sauce is consistency of thick cream. Serve piping hot over blind finches.

Birds' Nests

Netherlands-American Resource Center, Holland, Michigan

1 lb. ground or chopped beef	pepper, salt, nutmeg to taste
1 Tbsp. onion, finely chopped	2 Tbsp. butter or margarine
1 Tbsp. finely chopped parsley	4 eggs

Mix meat with onion, parsley and seasonings. Divide into four equal portions and shape into rings. Heat butter in large skillet and brown the rings on one side. Turn. Break one egg into each, taking care that the egg whites do not spill over the meat. Cover, and fry over moderate heat until egg whites are firm.

Serving suggestion: Serve with creamed spinach and strips of bread, fried golden brown.

Hunting Dish

Gerry Van Klompenburg, Saskatoon, Saskatchewan, Canada, lives on an acreage where she and her husband raise animals, wheat and hay. Both are Dutch immigrants.

1 lb. stewing beef, cubed	water to cover
6 1/2 Tbsp. margarine	4 potatoes, cubed
1 large onion, chopped fine	4 apples, peeled and sliced
1 bay leaf or to taste	salt to taste
peppercorns	4 Dutch rusks, crumbled
4 cloves	1/4 cup butter

Brown meat in margarine. Add onion, spices, and water to cover. Simmer 1 hour. Remove bay leaf. Add potatoes and apples and continue to simmer 45 minutes. Liquid should be somewhat reduced. Remove from pan and place in a baking dish. Crumble Dutch rusks on top. Add dots of butter. Bake at low temperature for approximately 8 minutes until golden brown, or for 3 minutes in microwave oven. Serves 4.

Pork Stew
Cochtah

Evelyn Vander Ploeg of Oostburg, Wisconsin, is a fourth generation descendant of Dutch immigrants. Like many other Oostburg residents, she is active in Holland Days celebrated each summer in neighboring Cedar Grove. Although the word cochtah *does not appear in Dutch dictionaries, that is the name this dish has acquired among Oostburg's Dutch cc· ks.*

2 lbs. pork steak	1 large onion, diced
1/2 cup celery leaves, chopped	4 or 5 potatoes, diced
1 onion, chopped	salt
1/2 cabbage, shredded	pepper
6 or 7 carrots, diced	seasoned salt

Place pork steak, celery leaves and onion in saucepan. Cover with water and simmer until pork steak is tender. Remove meat from broth and cool. Remove fat and cut meat into pieces. Strain broth. Cool and skim fat from surface.In separate pan, cook vegetables until tender. Add skimmed broth and meat. Add salt, pepper and seasoned salt to taste. Serves 4-6.

"This tastes really good reheated on the second day," says Evelyn.

Scrapple
Balkenbrij

Launa Riepma, Oak Harbor, Washington, has Dutch ancestors, but she says, "I learned Dutch cooking when I married a man who wanted me to cook like his mother had cooked. When I make Scrapple, we take turns stirring it. It's good to have a helper for the stirring process because your arms really get tired."

1 beef heart	1 Tbsp. allspice
1 beef tongue	1 tsp. pepper
2 lbs. (or more) beef liver	water to cover
3 Tbsp. salt or to taste	6 to 8 cups flour

Cube meats and place in large pan. Add spices and enough water to almost cover. Cover pan and simmer 15 to 20 minutes, until meat is tender. Remove meat from pan, reserving liquid, and grind. Return ground meat to pan and bring mixture to boil. Sift in

(continued)

flour and stir until mixture is very stiff. Pat into loaf pans and refrigerate. When cool, slice thinly and fry in butter until crisp. Serve on hot buttered toast.

Note: Pork may be used in place of beef.

Fish Fillets

Strawtown Inn, Pella, Iowa

6 5-oz. sole fillets, 1/8-inch
    thick
1 Tbsp. fresh lemon juice
1 tsp. salt
3 Tbsp. butter
waxed paper
6 bacon slices
1 cup flour
1/4 tsp. dill seed

1/4 tsp. nutmeg
freshly ground pepper
1/4 cup grated Gouda cheese
1/3 cup soft, fresh bread
    crumbs
1/4 cup blanched almonds,
    grated
3 Tbsp. chilled butter

Pat fillets dry. Sprinkle both sides with lemon juice and salt. Let stand at room temperature 30 minutes. Spread 2 tablespoons softened butter over bottom and sides of a shallow baking dish, large enough to hold the fish in one layer. Cut piece of waxed paper and fit snugly inside baking dish. Spread 1 tablespoon softened butter over top of paper. Set aside.

Fry bacon strips over moderate heat until nearly crisp. Drain on paper towels. Pat fillets dry and fold lengthwise in half. Press edges together to hold shape. Dip fillets in flour and gently shake off excess. Sprinkle both sides with dill seeds and nutmeg. Arrange side by side in buttered baking dish. Place a strip of bacon atop each one. Grind a little pepper over the top. Combine cheese, bread crumbs and almonds. Scatter the mixture evenly over the fish. Dot with bits of chilled butter. Bake in upper third of oven at 500°F. for 10 minutes, or until topping is brown and fish flakes easily. Serve immediately.

Dover Sole
Gebakken Zeetong

4 whole sole	flour
4 large beefsteak tomatoes	4 Tbsp. capers
1 cup butter	juice of 2 lemons
salt and pepper	1/4 cup white wine

Clean sole and remove skin. Dip tomatoes, one at a time, into boiling water for 30 seconds to loosen skin; peel and cut into equal wedges.

Clarify butter by heating very slowly; with a spoon, dip up clear oil that floats on top and put into frying pan. Discard remainder. Season sole with salt and pepper to taste and sprinkle lightly with flour. Over medium heat, fry sole in clarified butter until golden brown on both sides and done. Remove sole to serving platter and keep warm. Drain fat from pan; add tomato wedges, capers, lemon juice and white wine, and just heat through. Serve over the sole. Serves 4.

Fish Balls
Vis Ballen

Margie Kolean-Knol of Holland, Michigan, compiled a collection of Dutch and American recipes, "A Bit of Old Holland". This recipe is from her book. Margie is a secretary of Holland's Dutch Village, an amusement park featuring such Dutch attractions as wooden-shoed dancers, Dutch street organs and replicas of Netherlands buildings.

1 1/2 cups boned, cooked fish, reserve stock	1 egg, beaten
	1/4 tsp. pepper
1 cup soft bread crumbs	1/2 tsp. salt
2 Tbsp. minced onion	fish stock to cover
1/4 cup grated carrot	2 Tbsp. flour
1/2 tsp. sugar	1/2 cup minced parsley

Mix first 8 ingredients and roll into small balls. Heat fish stock to boiling, drop in fish balls and cook gently for 45 minutes.

(continued)

boiling, drop in fish balls and cook gently for 45 minutes. Remove balls from stock. Thicken stock with flour mixed with a little cold water. Add parsley and pour over fish balls. Chill well. Serve cold. Makes about 12.

Shrimp Croquettes
Garnalencroquetten

Shrimp croquettes are a favorite party food of M.J. Gertrude Reichenbach of Philadelphia, Pennsylvania. Director of the Dutch Studies Program at the University of Pennsylvania, she is a native of Heerlen, Netherlands. She has been a teacher in the United States since 1955. An honorary member of the Netherlands Society of Philadelphia, she received the John Adams Medal from the Netherlands government for her work on the American Bicentennial celebration.

3 Tbsp. butter	1 egg yolk
3 Tbsp. flour	1/4 cup heavy cream
1 cup boiling milk	2 cups minced large shrimp
1/2 cup concentrated	or tiny whole shrimp
shrimp stock	dry bread crumbs, as needed
1 Tbsp. chopped parsley	1 egg, beaten
salt	1 Tbsp. water
pepper	oil for deep frying
lemon juice to taste	parsley sprigs

Melt butter in a two-quart saucepan. Stir in flour. Gradually add milk and shrimp stock. Simmer, stirring constantly, until mixture forms a thick white sauce. Add chopped parsley and season to taste with salt, pepper and lemon juice. Beat egg yolk and cream in a bowl. Slowly add sauce to it. Return mixture to pan. Return to a boil, stirring constantly, until very thick. Fold in shrimp. Spread onto large, shallow platter and refrigerate.

When firm enough to handle, cut rectangles and shape into *croquettes*. Roll in bread crumbs. Mix egg and water.Roll *croquettes* in egg-water mixture. Roll them again in bread crumbs. (*Croquettes* should be well covered with crumbs.) Chill again.

Heat oil to 380°F. Fry, a few at a time, until golden. Drain on paper. Serve piping hot with parsley sprigs that have been dipped in hot oil for 30 seconds.

Potato-Sauerkraut Dish

Janni Drooger, Terrace, British Columbia

1 lb. sauerkraut
3 onions, chopped fine
6 Tbsp. butter or margarine,
    divided
1 lb. ground beef
2 tsp. curry powder
salt and pepper to taste

6 slices bacon, cut into
    1-inch slices
1 (8-oz.) can pineapple chunks
3 bananas, sliced
4 cups beef broth
6 potatoes, cooked, mashed,
    and seasoned

Drain and cut sauerkraut with kitchen shears. Fry onions in 4 tablespoons butter. Add ground beef and fry, stirring with fork. Add curry powder, salt and pepper. Line an oven dish with the bacon pieces. Add the beef and onion, then the sauerkraut. On top of this place pineapple and banana pieces. Pour broth over all. Spread mashed potatoes on top. Dot with 2 tablespoons butter.

If desired, some mashed potatoes may be reserved, placed in a pastry bag, and used to create decorative figures atop the casserole.

Bake at 350°F. for 50 minutes; broil an additional 10 minutes. Serves 4-6.

They Said It

There are many old sayings about Dutch cooks. One of them is that every Dutch recipe begins with the instruction, "Pour a jigger of brandywine into the cook." Another, "Not everyone is a cook who carries a long knife."

The Dutch Oven

The Dutch oven was brought to America from the Netherlands by early settlers, and has never lost its popularity. If it is a deep cooking pot, made of iron, with a tight-fitting, dome-shaped lid, it is a Dutch oven.

Dutch Farmer's Meal
Boerenspijs

June Van Dyke of Radnor, Pennsylvania, says, "My husband is of Dutch descent and I am too, so we're interested in all sorts of Dutch things." June learned this recipe for a complete meal in the home of Dien Pieper, a housewife, teacher and community worker in Harderwijk, Holland.

Buttermilk Dressing:

4 oz. smoked bacon	1 qt. buttermilk
3/8 cup flour	1/4 to 1 tsp. salt

Dice bacon and fry in deep pan on low heat until crisp. Remove bacon and place in small bowl for serving. Add flour to pan all at once. Stir. Add buttermilk in small amounts. To prevent curdling, keep mixture boiling as you add buttermilk. Stir constantly. Continue adding buttermilk until dressing reaches consistency of medium white sauce. Salt to taste. Serve dressing very warm.

Meal ingredients:

6 servings of lettuce leaves, broken into pieces	small bowl of fried bacon
	buttermilk dressing
small bowl of sliced onions	6 servings boiled potatoes
small bowl of chopped chives	small bowl of chopped
6 hard-cooked eggs, sliced	parsley (optional)

To eat a Dutch farmer's meal, each person beds his or her plate with fresh lettuce, sliced onions, chives, sliced eggs and bacon. Top with buttermilk dressing. Place boiled potatoes atop the mixture. Add more dressing.

June advises, "Each person takes as much dressing as desired, but you need a lot to make it tasty. We like parsley, so I include a small bowl of chopped parsley to top the meal." She adds that in Holland it is traditional for each person to take only one large serving.

Beef and Egg Sandwich
Uitsmijter

Uitsmijter *is one of the Dutch specialties featured at the Queen's Inn Restaurant in Holland, Michigan. Ceiling beams inscribed with Dutch proverbs, copper kettles and Delft tile create an Old World atmosphere in this restaurant that features both Dutch foods and traditional American favorites.*

Uitsmijter *is a popular and inexpensive sandwich at Netherlands' restaurants. As popular with the Dutch as the hamburger is with Americans, it is especially popular among business people needing a speedy lunch.*

2 slices white bread, buttered	2 eggs
medium-rare cold roast beef, thinly sliced, or cold ham, thinly sliced	sweet gherkin pickles

Cover buttered bread with roast beef or ham. Fry eggs, sunny-side up and place atop meat. Service open-faced with sweet gherkin pickles. Serve open-faced.

Potatoes and Kale
Stamppot met Boerenkool

Jacobina Veldman, who emigrated from the Netherlands in 1951, lives in Hollandale, Minnesota. Her main interests are sewing and crafts. "Stamppot met boerenkool is a very common dish in the northern part of Holland," she says. "We serve it in Hollandale for the annual Dutch supper in our church."

2 to 3 lbs. potatoes	1/4 cup butter
1/2 lb. fresh or frozen kale	1 tsp. salt
3 to 4 cups water	

Peel potatoes and place in 3-quart saucepan. Large potatoes should be cut in half. Remove large veins from fresh kale, simmer in separate saucepan for 10 minutes, drain, squeeze out excess water and cut fine. Place cut kale atop potatoes. If using frozen kale, simply cut fine and place it atop the potatoes.

Add water and simmer 1 hour. Add butter and salt and mash with potato masher. Add more water if necessary. Makes 6 servings. (continued)

Variations: "This is really good," Jacobina says, "when you put a ring bologna on top of the potatoes and kale before the 1-hour simmering." She adds, "Instead of kale, you can use carrots, white cabbage, French-cut beans, even sweet apples."
Betty Van Andel of Ada, Michigan, suggests applesauce as a delicious side dish to this. "We like boerenkool anytime — specially on a cold winter evening."

Bacon-Wrapped Muffin Loaf
Poffert

Jennie Veltkamp of Belgrade, Montana, learned of this dish from her Dutch mother. "We used to make this for a main meal at home, especially on Saturday."

1 lb. bacon	2 cups flour
1/4 cup butter or margarine	3 tsp, baking powder
1/4 cup sugar	3/4 cup milk
1 egg, well-beaten	

White sauce:

2 cups milk	1/2 cup sugar
2 Tbsp. cornstarch	1 tsp. vanilla
1 Tbsp. margarine	

Fry bacon until about half done. Line bottom of Bundt pan with enough bacon strips to cover. Cream butter and sugar. Add egg. Sift flour and baking powder. Add to first mixture alternately with milk. Pour into lined pan. Top with remaining bacon. Bake at 350° F. for 30 to 45 minutes.

Mix white sauce ingredients in saucepan and bring to a boil, stirring constantly. Remove from heat when mixture thickens. Cut muffin loaf into serving-sized pieces and top with white sauce. Serves 4.

Variation: *Poffert* may be baked in 2 loaf pans instead of in a Bundt pan. For a larger loaf, double the recipe.

Breads, Porridges, and Pancakes

Breads, not boxed cereals, are the filling staple at the Dutch breakfast table. Pancakes are served as snacks, desserts and main dishes, but not for breakfast. Dutch breads and cakes of all varieties are a special delight whenever they are served.

Currant Bread
Krentenbrood

Alice Slager Kuiper and her husband, Bill, farm near Racine, Wisconsin. Alice says, "I was born and raised on a farm, married a farmer in 1942, and we have farmed since 1950. My interests are baking, flower gardens and vegetable and fruit gardens."

Currant bread is a delicacy on a traditional Dutch koffietafel. Custom requires that guests limit themselves to one slice of it. It is usually eaten last as a special treat to end the meal.

1 3/4 cup warm milk	1/4 cup lukewarm water
3 Tbsp. butter	5 cups flour
3 Tbsp. sugar	2 cups currants
1 egg	1 cup raisins
1/2 tsp. salt	3 Tbsp. candied lemon
2 pkgs. yeast	peel, chopped (optional)

Mix milk, butter, sugar, egg and salt. Mix yeast in water. Let stand 5 to 10 minutes until dissolved. Add to first mixture. Gradually add flour. Knead. Cover and let stand in a warm place for 1 hour. Punch down and add currants, raisins and lemon peel. Shape into 2 loaves. Place in greased and floured loaf pans. Cover with damp cloth and let rise again in warm place for 1 hour. Bake at 350°F. for 1 hour or until brown.

Rye Bread
Roggebrood

Ladonna Van Klomperburg Huisman, who lives on a farm near Hospers, Iowa, is active in the annual Tulip Festival at nearby Orange City. Her great-grandfather, Everett Bloemendaal, emigrated from the Dutch province of Gelderland in 1867. He wrote a diary of his experiences in the United States, "Naar Amerika" (My America), which was published for Dutchmen considering emigration. It was later translated into English, and a limited edition was published for his descendants.

3 cups rye meal
1 cup flour
1 tsp. salt

1 tsp. baking soda
1/2 cup dark corn syrup
1 cup sour milk or buttermilk

Mix ingredients and pour into 2 loaf-sized bread pans. Place pans in flat cake pans (e.g. 13x9-inch) in the oven. Add water to pan and steam breads at 250°F. for 3 hours. When cool, slice and serve with butter.

Rye Bread II
Roggebrood

Dorothy Roeters, who came to the United States when she was seven, is at home with food preparation. Now retired and living in Grand Rapids, Michigan, she previously worked as a caterer for several years and spent a decade managing a small restaurant.

2 cups rye grits*
1 cup white flour
1/2 cup brown sugar
1 tsp. salt

2 cups buttermilk
1 rounded tsp. baking soda
2 Tbsp. dark molasses
2 Tbsp. vegetable oil

Mix first 4 ingredients in large mixing bowl. In smaller bowl mix buttermilk and baking soda. Add molasses and oil. Add this mixture to the first bowl. Mix well, but do not beat. Pour into greased bread pan. Let set 1/2 hour. Bake in preheated oven 1 hour at 350°F. Remove from oven and cover with another bread pan, inverted. Remove from pan when cold.

Note: Dorothy advises wrapping this rye bread in waxed paper rather than plastic wrap and storing it in the refrigerator after the first day—if there's any left! Tastes good served with cheese.

*Rye grits are available at health food stores.

Grandma's Graham Bread
Authentieke Volkorenbrood

Lois Plaggemars Knoll, who lives in Holland, Michigan, works at a candle shop on Windmill Island, Holland's municipal park featuring a magnificent Dutch windmill, De Zwaan.

1 pt. sour milk or buttermilk	1 1/3 tsp. baking soda
2 1/2 cups graham flour	1 tsp. salt
1/3 cup brown sugar	nuts and/or raisins as desired

Mix ingredients together to form a stiff batter. Pour into well-greased loaf pan. Bake at 350°F. for 50 minutes.

Barley and Raisin Stew
Moesgoed

Junior high teacher Ann Fisher of Wyckoff, New Jersey, enjoyed moesgoed *in the home of her parents, the late Bertha and Bastian Vande Ree. Ann's brother Case recalls, "Moesgoed was a heavy, porridge-type food we ate for supper. Served hot, it was great. Served cold just before bedtime, it was even better."*

1 cup barley	1/4 to 1/2 cup chopped
1 quart buttermilk	mint leaves
1 1-lb. pkg. raisins	2 or 3 slices bacon or cubed
	ham (optional)

Rinse barley; place in kettle and cover with water. Bring to rapid boil. Remove from heat and let stand in covered kettle 1 hour. Barley will greatly expand.

Add buttermilk and return to heat. Simmer, stirring occasionally, 1 1/2 hours or until done. Add raisins, mint and ham (if desired) during the cooking. If bacon is desired, fry crisp and crumble over *moesgoed*. Serve hot or cold with dark corn syrup. Serves 6.

Oatmeal
Havermoutpap

Dr. Benjamin Spock is best known for his book, "The Common Sense Book of Baby and Child Care". He is a descendant of Dutch immigrant James Spaak who served in the American Revolution. He noted, "I cook and eat steel-cut oatmeal every day."

2 cups water   dash salt
1/2 cup steel-cut oats

Combine above ingredients and cook over low heat for 30 minutes. Serve with cream and maple syrup.

Steamed Pudding
Jan-in-de-zak

Cornelia Flikkema of Manhattan, Montana, serves Jan-in-de-zak *to her family as a complete meal. "It is our family favorite," she says. "Even my sons and daughters-in-law have learned to like it!"*

Often served on New Year's Eve in the Netherlands, Jan-in-de-zak *is a close relative of the English plum pudding.*

Jan-in-de-zak, *which means literally "Jack in the sack," gets its name from the way it is prepared — suspended in a sack. As it bounces around in the boiling water,* Jan-in-de-zak *does seem to have life.*

In Dutch tradition, half of the batter is prepared in a sack and half in a double boiler as a kettle-cake. Jan-in-de-zak *keeps peeping over the edge of his pan to watch over his little brother, kettle-cake.*

2 cups white flour   2 eggs
1 cup buckwheat flour   2 tsp. baking powder
3/4 cup sugar   2 cups milk

Mix all ingredients together until well blended. Put into a cloth sack, leaving room for expansion. Fill a large pan half full of water. When it begins to boil, place sack in water. Boil for 2 hours, turning sack every half-hour.

Serve sliced, topped with fried bacon bits, bacon grease, and brown sugar or syrup.

Alternate method: Grease and flour several cans. Fill each can half full of batter and cover with foil. Set cans in pans of water and bake at 350°F. for 2 hours. Batter can also be baked on top of stove in this manner. Serves 4.

144

Currant Porridge
Krentenbrij

Writer Peter De Vries remembers with nostalgia the dishes his Dutch mother made when he was growing up in Chicago. He writes, "Moes, a dish of stewed greens and potatoes, was a staple among our Chicago Dutch folk, and so was something we called poteten, *mostly mashed turnips and any number of optionals, which was a hearty dinner favorite. Every Saturday we had our* krentenbrook *(currant bread), of course, and there was a soup made of currants and barley, which I wish I had a bowl of right now. Good old* krentenbrij.*"*

An editor for "The New Yorker" and a novelist, Peter De Vries lives in Westport, Connecticut.

1/4 lb. currants	1/4 tsp. cinnamon
1/4 lb. barley	4 quarts water
1/4 lb. brown sugar	1 pt. grape juice

Mix currants, barley, brown sugar, cinnamon and water. Simmer for 1 1/2 hours. Add grape juice. Simmer for an additional 1/2 hour. Makes 4 quarts.

Buttermilk Porridge
Karnemelkpap

Margret Bloemendaal Rutgers of Lynden, Washington, enjoys this simple, old-fashioned porridge recipe.

1/2 cup barley	3 cups water
1/2 tsp. salt	1 1/2 quarts buttermilk

Cook barley, salt and water in double boiler until well done. Add more water if needed before cooking is complete. Cool to luke-warm. Drain.

Place barley in heavy pan to prevent scorching. Add buttermilk a little at a time, stirring constantly. Heat mixture just to a boil. Serve with sugar or syrup.

Alternate method: If you want to refrigerate *karnemelkpap*, stir 2 tablespoons flour into barley just before adding buttermilk. This will keep buttermilk from separating when the porridge is refrigerated. It can be stored a few days. Serves 6-8.

Pancakes
Flensjes

A recipe for flensjes *(large, thin pancakes) was among those found by Cornelia (Nella) Breugem Kennedy in the vault of the Dutch Heritage room at Northwestern College in Orange City, Iowa. Nella is an archivist.*

4 cups milk	4 Tbsp. shortening
2 cups flour	4 eggs
4 Tbsp. sugar	

Lightly beat all ingredients together. Pour a very thin layer of batter across the bottom of a large greased frying pan. Brown lightly on both sides. Turn *flensjes* carefully. Remove to warm platter. Spread with butter, then sugar and cinnamon mixture, jelly, preserves, or sugar moistened with orange juice, or other flavor. Roll up with forks. Serve hot. Serves 4.

Mini-Pancakes
Pella Poffertjes

Poffertjes *are a Dutch treat that Pella, Iowa, serves to its Tulip Festival visitors each year. The tiny pancakes are prepared by the Pella Kiwanis Clubs and the Pella Historical Society on* poffertje *grills imported from the Netherlands.*

1 cup flour	3 eggs
4 Tbsp. sugar	4 Tbsp. vegetable oil
1 tsp. salt	butter
1 cup hot tap water	powdered sugar

Mix flour, sugar and salt. Add water, eggs and oil. Mix well until batter is lump-free. Fry on *poffertjes* grill or fry silver-dollar-sized pancakes in frying pan. To serve, spread with butter and sprinkle with powdered sugar.

Desserts

Apple Balls

Tet Tacoma-Doornbos of Guelph, Ontario, Canada, says, "My father used to be a pastry chef in Holland. Every time he comes to Canada he makes several dozen Apple Balls for us."

1 1/3 cups flour	8 medium-sized apples
1 cup margarine	1 cup sugar
3 Tbsp. water	2 Tbsp. cinnamon
dash of salt	1 egg
1/2 to 3/4 cup flour to dust work counter	8 baking cups

In large bowl combine sifted flour, margarine, water and salt. Cut margarine through flour with two knives until dough sticks together. Do not knead. Roll dough on floured work surface. It will be very sticky, but keep sprinkling with flour as you roll. Roll dough into large square. Fold to four thicknesses. Let rest for 20 minutes. Roll to large square again. Fold to four thicknesses, and again let rest 20 minutes.

In the meantime, peel and core the apples. Mix sugar and cinnamon in small bowl. In separate bowl, slightly beat egg for sealing and brushing.

Roll dough out on floured board to 1/4-inch thickness. Cut 8 5x5-inch squares. Place a cored apple in center of square. Fill hollow center with sugar and cinnamon mixture. Fold dough to cover apple completely. If it does not stay together, moisten edges. Turn apple over into baking cup, with folded dough on the bottom.

Brush with egg. Let stand 10 minutes. Brush again with egg. Bake at 400°F. for 15 minutes and at 450°F. for another 5 minutes, until golden brown. Check with fork to see if the apples are done. **Note:** Unbaked, and without egg brushed on, these freeze well. When you take them out of freezer, brush on egg and bake a little longer. Muffin tins, aluminum foil cups, or a pan may be used.

Brown Betty

Dutch Heritage Collection at Northwestern College, Orange City, Iowa

6 large apples
5 rusks or slices dry bread, cubed
1/2 cup sugar

1/2 cup butter or margarine
3/4 tsp. cinnamon
3 eggs

Peel, core, slice and cook apples in a little water until they form a sauce. Add rusk (or bread) cubes, sugar, butter and cinnamon. In a separate bowl, beat eggs. Fold into apple mixture. Bake in buttered 13x9-inch pan at 350°F. until top is brown, about 20 minutes.

Meringue Compote

Netherlands Ministry of Agriculture and Fisheries

1 lb. 10 oz. stewed rhubarb
   or gooseberries
2 eggs

1/4 cup sugar
2 tsp. powdered sugar

Separate egg yolks and whites. Mix stewed fruit with yolks and put in a greased ovenproof dish. Beat egg whites until stiff. Add sugar and beat a little longer. Spoon meringue over fruit and sprinkle with powdered sugar. Bake at 400°F. until meringue is light brown. Serves 4.

Orange Moss

Trene Leegwater of Midland Park, New Jersey. Before moving to New Jersey, the Leegwaters operated a bulb and flower farm in North Carolina.

1 package lemon gelatin
1 1/2 cups boiling water
2 Tbsp. sugar

1/2 cup orange juice
1 Tbsp. orange rind, grated
1 cup whipping cream

Dissolve gelatin in boiling water. Add sugar, orange juice and grated rind. Chill until syrupy. Whip cream until thick and shiny, but not stiff. Fold into gelatin. Chill until firm. Serves 6 to 8.

Applesauce and Cream with Rusks

Netherlands Ministry of Agriculture and Fisheries

4 rusks	1 cup whipping cream
1 cup applesauce	sugar to taste

Place 1 rusk in each of 4 small serving bowls. Top each with 1/4 cup applesauce. Let soak well into the rusk. Whip cream and sweeten to taste. Before serving, decorate rusks with the whipped cream.

Dutch Treat

Mina Baker-Roelofs, Pella, Iowa

Crust:

(1) 5-oz. package rusks	1/2 cup sugar
1/2 cup butter	

Filling:

3/4 cup sugar	3 1/2 cups scalded milk
6 Tbsp. cornstarch	4 egg yolks
1/2 tsp. salt	1 tsp. vanilla

Meringue:

4 egg whites	1/2 cup sugar
3/4 tsp. cream of tartar	1/4 cup nut meats, broke

Crust: Roll rusks very fine and mix with butter and sugar. Set aside 1/4 of mixture and use remaining 3/4 to line 9-inch spring-form pan (without center tube). Press crumbs in firmly.

Filling: Mix sugar, cornstarch and salt. Add milk gradually, stirring constantly. Cook in double boiler for 18 minutes, stirring until thickened. Beat egg yolks slightly. Pour part of hot mixture over them, mixing well. Return this to double boiler. Cook about 2 minutes longer, stirring constantly. Remove from heat. Stir in vanilla. Pour into crumb-lined pan.

Meringue: Beat egg whites until foamy. Sprinkle cream of tartar over them and beat until stiff. Beat in sugar gradually. Spread over cream filling and sprinkle with nuts and reserved crumb mixture.Bake at 325°F. about 15 minutes, until delicately browned. Serve cold. Serves 8.

Buttermilk and Strawberries

Netherlands Ministry of Agriculture and Fisheries

4 pints buttermilk

4 Dutch rusks

brown sugar to taste

1 cup fresh strawberries

Rinse a clean closely woven towel; place it in a colander and set in a deep bowl. Pour buttermilk into the towel and cover; scrape and stir from time to time to allow whey to drip freely. The process takes time. Start early. Discard the whey. Scrape the resulting thick, yogurt-like cream into a bowl. Whip to eliminate lumps. Chill. Spoon buttermilk cream into 4 bowls. Crumble a Dutch rusk over each. Top with strawberries and brown sugar to taste.
Note: The Dutch name for this summer dessert is *"Hangop"* (hanged). The name is derived from a practice of Dutch country folk who hung the buttermilk in a pillowcase from a branch to allow the whey to drip.

Limburg Fruit Tart

Netherlands Ministry of Agriculture and Fisheries. Limburg Fruit Tart is named for a Netherlands province where this pastry is a specialty.

2 1/4 cups flour

1/4 cup sugar

1 tsp. salt

1/4 cup milk

(1) 1 oz. cake yeast

1/4 cup butter

1 egg

2 lbs. 2 oz. sliced peaches, apricots, or other fresh and/or stewed fruit

2 tsp. sugar

Mix flour, 1/4 cup sugar and salt in large bowl. Heat milk to luke-warm. Stir yeast, butter and egg into milk. Stir into flour mixture. Knead. Cover and let rise in warm place 1 hour. Roll 3/4 of dough to fit 10-inch-round deep, greased baking dish.

Place fruit slices overlapping each other on dough, in two layers. Roll out remaining dough and cut into strips. Lay the strips crisscross over the fruit. Brush sides and strips of tart with lightly beaten egg. Bake at 400°F. for 30 minutes, or until fruit is cooked and pastry is lightly browned. Sprinkle with 2 tsp. sugar immediately after removing from oven.

Rice with Currants and Raisins

Netherlands Ministry of Agriculture and Fisheries

1 cup uncooked rice
2 2/3 cups water
1 tsp. salt

3/4 cup currants
3/4 cup raisins
butter and sugar to taste

Wash rice. Place in saucepan with water and salt. Wash currants and raisins and place on top of rice. Simmer until rice is cooked. Stir currants and raisins carefully into rice. Serve with butter and sugar.

Rice Pudding

Chamber of Commerce, Pella, Iowa

1/4 cup uncooked long grain rice
1 cup water
2 cups milk
1/4 tsp. salt
1/2 cup sugar
1 tsp. grated lemon rind
1 tsp. vanilla

1/4 tsp. nutmeg
1 Tbsp. butter
2 eggs, slightly beaten
1/4 cup raisins
1 Tbsp. fine, dry bread
    crumbs
fruit optional

In saucepan bring rice and water to a boil. Drain. Scald milk in top of double boiler. Add rice and salt, and cook 20 minutes, or until rice is almost tender, stirring occasionally. Remove from heat.

Mix sugar, lemon rind, vanilla, nutmeg, butter, eggs and raisins. Add mixture to rice.

Butter a 1-quart casserole and sprinkle with bread crumbs. Pour in rice mixture. Set in a pan of hot water and bake at 350°F. for 1 hour, or until pudding is rather firm and lightly browned. Cool and serve. Top with fruit if desired.

Hague's Bluff

Mrs. Harmen Doornbos, Abbotsford, British Columbia, uses this traditional Dutch recipe to top puddings and gelatins.

3 egg whites   2 Tbsp. sugar
1 cup of any fruit juice

Beat ingredients together in large bowl until thick and fluffy. Serves 6.

Rice Pancakes

Netherlands-American Resource Center, Holland, Michigan

2 eggs, separated   2 1/2 cups cold, cooked rice
1/3 cup sugar   1/2 cup flour
cinnamon to taste   2 to 4 Tbsp. butter

Beat egg yolks with sugar and cinnamon until light and fluffy. Beat egg whites. Fold in the rice, flour and beaten egg whites, in that order, into the egg yolk mixture. In hot butter, fry tablespoonfuls of this mixture to a golden brown, taking care that they remain round and separate. Turn when tops begin to dry. Serve hot, sprinkled with a mixture of sugar and cinnamon. Approximately 10 cakes.

Chocolate Pudding

Margaret Kleis of Holland, Michigan, says, "When I grew up in the Netherlands in the 1930s and 40s, flavored gelatin and flavored pudding mixes were unknown. Besides cornstarch, we sometimes used flour, Cream of Wheat or oats for thickening."

1/3 cup sugar or honey   2 cups milk
2 Tbsp. cornstarch   1 tsp. vanilla
2 Tbsp. cocoa   1/4 cup peanut butter

Combine sugar or honey, cornstarch and cocoa. Slowly stir in milk. Cook over low heat until thick, stirring constantly. Remove from heat. Add vanilla and peanut butter. Serve hot or cold. Serves 6.
Note: Margaret's grandchildren prefer smooth peanut butter.

Cookies and Candy
Koekjes en Babbelaars

Dutch cookies are a dieter's downfall. Rich, buttery and spicy, they are one of my favorite Dutch specialties. When I was a youngster, "Windmill Cookies" from the Orange City, Iowa, bakery made any day special. (I later learned that they were more widely known as *speculaas* and could be molded into other shapes as well.) Almond-sprinkled *Janhagels* were good, too. But none, of course, could top the delectable crispness of my Dutch grandmother's sugar cookies. —Carol Van Klompenburg

Almond Paste Cookies

Bertha Van Klompenburg, Orange City, Iowa

2 egg whites, unbeaten   1 cup almond paste
1 cup sugar

Stir together all ingredients. Drop walnut-sized balls of mixture onto greased cookie sheet. Bake at 325°F. for 25 minutes. Remove promptly from cookie sheet to prevent sticking.

Dutch Handkerchiefs

Esther Roorda, Pella, Iowa

Crust:
2 cups flour   1/4 cup water
1 cup butter or margarine

Filling:
1 egg white   1 tsp. almond flavoring
1 cup sugar

Crust: Cut butter into flour until well-blended. Add water 1 tablespoonful at a time. Roll crust thin. Cut into 4-inch squares.
Filling: Beat egg white until stiff. Fold in sugar and almond flavoring. Put 1 teaspoon of filling in center of each square and fold crust corners to center. Bake at 350°F. until lightly browned.

Dutch Letters

Eunice Robijn De Soto of Tacoma, Washington, is the great-granddaughter of a Friesland baker. She says: "This recipe has been used in our family especially for Christmas. The strips are formed into the shape of the first letter of your last name or of your friends. Then give for a gift, as was done traditionally in Holland." Eunice suggests serving Dutch Letters with milk tea as her grandmother did.

Almond Paste:

4 eggs	2 to 3 cups powdered sugar
2 tsp. almond flavoring	1 1/2 cups almonds, chopped fine

Pastry:

1 1/4 cups lard or shortening	pinch of salt
2 cups flour	3 Tbsp. water

Filling: Beat eggs, saving the white of one egg. Stir in almond flavoring. Add powdered sugar and almonds. Refrigerate 2 hours or overnight.

Pastry: Blend lard or shortening, flour and salt with pastry blender. Stir in water, 1 tablespoonful at a time. Roll out on lightly floured board and cut into 4-inch-wide strips. Place almond paste along center of each strip, and fold over the dough. To seal, moisten the long edge of each strip with egg white.

Length of individual filled strips will be determined by size of letters to be shaped. Cut filled strips, seal ends and place strips on cookie sheet, seam side down. Form into letters, pressing edges securely together. Brush tops with lightly beaten egg white.

Bake at 425°F. for 10 minutes. Prick holes in top of each letter and return to oven. Bake at 350°F. an additional 15 minutes, or until lightly browned. Letters may be topped with powdered sugar icing, if desired.

Sand Cookies

Connie Walraven, Georgetown, Ontario, Canada

1 cup butter
2/3 cup brown sugar
2/3 cup white sugar
1 egg

2 cups flour
1/2 tsp. baking soda
1/2 tsp. almond extract or
    2 tsp. vanilla

Cream butter and sugars together. Add egg and mix well with wooden spoon. Add flour and baking soda. Add almond extract or vanilla and mix well. Drop approximately 1 heaping tablespoonful into each greased muffin tin. Bake at 350°F. for 18 minutes. Makes 12.

Spice Cookies
Speculaas Koekjes

Thirteen-year-old Lisa Jaarsma of Pella, Iowa, says, "I brought these cookies to the Marion County fair, where I received a top ribbon for them. From there they went to the Iowa State Fair where I received a blue ribbon and the special Meredith Award for them." Lisa adapted this recipe from one used by the first settlers of Pella. Lisa's father Ralph owns Pella's Jaarsma Bakery, which features many traditional Dutch pastries. "Even though I don't have to," says Lisa, "I love to cook and bake." Her goal is to make her recipes taste as good as her father's.

These cookies are usually formed in cookie board molds. Traditionally in the shape of St. Nicholas, they're often called "St. Nick" cookies.

2 cups brown sugar
1 1/2 cups butter
3 1/2 cups flour
1 egg, beaten
1 tsp. baking powder
1 scant tsp. salt

1 tsp. cinnamon
3/4 tsp. ground cloves
1/2 tsp. nutmeg
1/2 tsp. allspice
1/2 tsp. ginger

Cream butter and sugar. Add remaining ingredients and stir. Mixture will form a very stiff dough. Shape dough into cylinder with diameter equal to the desired cookie size and chill thoroughly in covered container. Slice. Place on cookie sheet and bake at 350°F. for 10 to 12 minutes. Store in sealed container to retain crispness. Makes 6 dozen.
Variation: Press well-chilled dough into molded cookie boards instead of slicing rolled dough.

Filled Spice Cookies
Gevulde Speculaas

This recipe is from Pinky Vander Griend Glass of Lynden, Washington, where her mother's family settled in 1901 after leaving Nebraska. "I am a third-generation member of the Vander Griend family," says Pinky. "We just had our annual picnic in July, with over 120 people attending!

Originally made in cookie molds, speculaas derived their name from the Latin word for mirror, because they were mirror images of the mold. American immigrant Dutch use the term for many spice cookies, whether or not they are molded.

4 cups flour	1 tsp. baking soda
1 lb. butter	1 tsp. cloves
1 cup brown sugar	1 tsp. allspice
3/4 cup granulated sugar	1/2 tsp. nutmeg
2 tsp. baking powder	2 Tbsp. milk
2 tsp. cinnamon	

Filling:

2 cups ground almonds (8 oz.)	3 eggs
1 1/2 cups sugar	2 Tbsp. lemon juice

Mix first 10 ingredients (up to the milk) and knead until dough forms a ball. Divide into 4 equal parts. Spread 2 parts in thin layers in two 13x9-inch pans. Mix filling ingredients. Spread half of filling mixture in each pan. Cover fillings with remaining parts of dough mixture. Sprinkle milk over each pan with a spoon. Bake at 375°F. for 20 to 30 minutes or until dough leaves sides of pan. Cut into squares when cool. Freezes well.

Variation: Prepared almond paste can be used instead of ground almonds, substituting 1/2 to 1 pound according to taste.

Figure Eight Cookies
Krakelingen

Jennie Vander Stad Sweetman lives in a stone country house near Warwick, New York, and writes a weekly column, "Down History's Lane," for the "New Jersey Herald."

1/2 lb. butter	3/4 cup water
1/2 lb. margarine	sugar
3 1/2 cups flour	

Cut butter and margarine into flour. Gradually stir in water. Chill. Form into strips 1/2 to 1/4 inch in diameter. Roll in sugar. Shape into figure-eights and flatten with rolling pin. Bake at 400°F. for 5 to 8 minutes.

Almond Paste Cookies
Gevulde Speculaas

Goy Hummel Drexhage of Ripon, California, makes gevulde speculaas *as a special treat for Saint Nicholas Day.*

Ripon junior high teacher Lorna Van Gilst says, "The Drexhages amaze people with the beauty of their yard and garden. They have done a great deal to help the Vietnamese refugees who were sponsored by our church some years ago."

Goy suggests serving gevulde speculaas *with tea or coffee.*

1/2 cup butter	1 egg
1/2 cup shortening	2 cups flour
1/2 cup granulated sugar	1/2 tsp. baking powder
1/2 cup brown sugar	

Filling:

1 cup almond paste	2 eggs
3/4 cup sugar	grated rind of 1 lemon

Cream butter, shortening and sugars. Add egg. Add flour and baking powder. In separate bowl, mix filling ingredients. Spread half of cake batter in 13x9-inch glass baking dish. Spread filling over batter in pan and cover with remaining batter. Bake 45 minutes at 300°F. Cool and cut into bars. Freezes well.

Grandma's Sugar Cookies
Uitstekende Suikerkoekjes

Marie (Mrs. John) Kiel of Orange City, Iowa, learned to make these cookies from her Dutch mother at the turn of the century. They were a favorite treat for her eleven children, and she often served them to grandchildren and great-grandchildren when they visited. She needed to keep an ample supply: on her ninetieth birthday her direct descendants totaled 144! She was a grandmother to "Delightfully Dutch" author Carol Van Klompenburg.

1/2 cup lard or shortening
1/2 cup margarine
1 1/2 cups sugar
1 egg
2 Tbsp. cream

1/4 tsp. vanilla
2 1/2 cups flour
2 tsp. baking powder
1/8 tsp. baking soda
pinch of salt

Cream shortening, margarine, and sugar. Stir in egg, cream and vanilla. Stir together dry ingredients and add. Blend well. Drop from teaspoons onto greased cookie sheet. Flatten cookies with a fork. Bake at 375°F. until the edges just begin to brown. Makes 5 dozen.

Dutch Refrigerator Cookies
Makkelijke Koekjes

Ann Batema, Holland, Michigan

1 cup shortening or margarine
1/2 cup granulated sugar
1/2 cup brown sugar
1 egg
2 1/4 cups flour
1/2 tsp. baking soda

1/2 tsp. salt
2 tsp. cinnamon
1/4 tsp. nutmeg
1/4 tsp. cloves
1/2 cup chopped walnuts

Cream together shortening and sugars. Add egg and beat well. Sift dry ingredients and stir into creamed mixture. Add nuts. Shape into rolls with 2 1/2-inch diameters. Wrap in waxed paper and chill thoroughly. Slice very thin and bake at 350° F. for 5 to 7 minutes on lightly greased cookie sheet. Makes 5-6 dozen.

Almond Cookies
Bitterkoekjes

Before moving to South Holland, Illinois, Winnie Niehof and her husband owned a bakery in Appingedam, Holland, for 20 years. Although they are retired, baking is still part of the family tradition. Their son-in-law now runs a bakery in South Holland.

1/2 lb. almond paste 3/4 cup sugar
2 egg whites, unbeaten

Mix ingredients together with a fork. Drop by teaspoon onto greased cookie sheet. Bake at 300° F. for 20 minutes. Remove from cookie sheet promptly to prevent sticking.

Goat Leg Cookies
Bokkepootjes

Mina Baker-Roelofs, a teacher of home economics at Central College in Pella, Iowa, was co-editor of the Pella Collector's Cookbook. *She has a special interest in Dutch foods and costumes.*

Traveling in the Netherlands, Mina found that bokkepootjes *were a special treat served by elegant Dutch restaurants. Mina also enjoyed these cookies at the Art Institute of Chicago reception for Queen Beatrix in the summer of 1982.*

3 egg whites apricot jam
1/2 cup sugar 1/2 lb. semisweet chocolate
1/2 cup finely ground squares
   almonds

Beat egg whites until stiff. Add sugar gradually. Add ground almonds to this meringue and put in cookie press. Shape cookies into ovals on baking sheet which has been covered with ungreased paper. Bake at once at 250° F. for 1 hour. (If allowed to stand before baking, cookies will lose their shape.) Remove from paper at once after baking is completed.

Just before serving, spread flat bottoms of cookies with apricot jam, and press bottoms together to make a filled cookie. Dip both ends of filled cookies in melted chocolate. Cool until chocolate hardens.

Variation: To make *bokkepootjes* which can be filled ahead of time and remain crisp, a powdered sugar icing may be used as a filling instead of apricot jam.

Almond Cookies
Janhagels

Helen Van Wesep DeVos of Grand Rapids, Michigan, says, "I graduated as an elementary school teacher from a local denominational college (Dutch, of course)." She is married to the co-founder and president of the Amway Corporation.

Janhagel (Johnny Buckshot) cookies are named after mercenary soldiers whom the Dutch hired and nicknamed Jan Hagels. *The term is so frequently used that it has become a common noun in the Dutch language.*

Sprinkled with nuts or almond slices, the cookies do look a bit as if they are covered with buckshot.

1 cup butter	pinch of salt
1 cup sugar	1/2 tsp. vanilla
1 egg, separated	2 tsp. water
2 cups sifted flour	1/2 to 1 cup chopped nuts or
1/2 tsp. cinnamon	almonds

Cream butter. Add sugar, then egg yolk; cream well. Sift dry ingredients. Add gradually to the first mixture. Add vanilla. Place mixture on greased 15x10-inch baking sheet. Press into even layer with fingers. Mix egg white and water. Brush onto cookie mixture. Sprinkle with nuts or sliced almonds. Bake at 300° F. for 1/2 hour. Cut in squares while slightly warm. Makes 5 to 6 dozen.

Butter Cookies
Boterkoekjes

Alyda De Stigter Kosters, a retired teacher in Sioux Center, Iowa, received this recipe from her aunt, who worked in the home of a wealthy Dutch family. Alyda says, "The recipe originally was measured in tablespoons, but when my aunt came to America in 1908 she changed it to cups." Alyda, who enjoys cooking and baking, finds the Old Dutch recipes are still her favorites.

1 3/4 cups butter (not margarine)	3 cups flour
1 cup sugar	

Bring butter to room temperature. Mix butter and sugar until thoroughly blended. Add four and mix well. Roll into balls the size of a walnut. Place on a greased cookie sheet and (continued) flatten with a glass dipped in milk. Bake at 300° F. for 15 to 20 minutes until edges just begin to brown. Watch carefully—cookies must not be brown. Recipe makes 40 large cookies that freeze well.

Alyda says, "Boterkoekjes make a delightful dessert served with vanilla ice cream and strawberries." She also uses this recipe to make valentine cookies, rolling out the dough and cutting it into heart shapes. After baking them, she decorates them with a pink, powdered sugar frosting.

Holland Jumbles
Onze Echte "Jumbles"

Frieda Den Ouden Muilenburg of Edgerton, Minnesota, says, "Dutch foods are not foreign to me because my father was born in the Netherlands and my mother was also of Dutch descent. In 1976 we were able to tour Holland and in 1971 we had an exchange student from there in our home for a number of months. The Muilenburgs were also of Dutch descent and were early settlers in the Pella area."

She adds, "I am all for keeping our Dutch heritage alive with the help of festivals, cookbooks or what have you." Edgerton sponsors a two-day Dutch festival each July.

1 cup sugar	1 cup milk, scalded and
1 cup flour	cooled
2 tsp. baking powder	2 egg whites, beaten stiff
pinch of salt	

Frosting:

4 Tbsp. butter	2 Tbsp. cream
2 cups powdered sugar	shredded coconut

Mix dry ingredients and sift seven times. (This is important.) Add the milk and fold in egg whites. Pour into a 13x9-inch, ungreased pan and bake at 350° F. for 30 minutes or until a toothpick inserted into the dough comes out clean. After baking, cut into 2x3-inch squares. Cool.

To make frosting, cream butter and sugar together. Add cream and blend into a smooth paste. Add more cream until mixture forms thin frosting. Dip squares in frosting, coating every side, then roll them in shredded coconut. Broil briefly until coconut browns.

Lace Cookies
Kletskopjes

Martha Lautenbach is curator of the Scholte House in Pella, Iowa. The seventeen-room mansion, built in 1848 by Pella's founder, H.P. Scholte, retains many of the furnishings of its original owners.

Martha's recipe for kletskopjes *is the Dutch recipe friends and acquaintances most frequently ask her to share. She translated it from an old Dutch cookbook.*

scant 1/2 cup butter	1/2 cup flour
(not margarine)	1/2 cup slivered almonds
1 1/4 cups brown sugar	

Soften butter. Blend with brown sugar. Add flour and almonds. Stir with fork until mixture forms a ball. Drop onto baking sheet, using only 1 level teaspoon of dough for each cookie. Do not put more than 12 on a baking sheet because dough spreads. Bake at 350° F. for 5 to 6 minutes, or until bubbly all over. Remove from oven and watch carefully until you can just lift or slide cookies from sheet with thin spatula. Transfer to a cold baking sheet until crisp. Store in covered tin box. Makes 6 dozen.

The Strawtown Inn at Pella, Iowa, developed by the Stu Kuypers and the Bob Kleins, features dining in an Old World atmosphere, where Dutch delicacies are served.

Cakes and Pastries
Gebak en Nagerecht

Rich Dutch pastries like *oliebollen* and *banket* are luscious and addicting. A diner is always tempted to try just one more. Apples and almonds are popular in the recipes of Dutch Americans, especially in their pastries and desserts.

Dutch Apple Cake

Mina Baker-Roelofs of Pella, Iowa.

1 cup milk	1 pkg. of cake yeast
1/2 cup sugar	1 egg
1 tsp. salt	4 cups unsifted flour
1/2 cup (1 stick) butter	6 cups apple slices, drained
1/4 cup warm water, 105°-115°	(2 1-lb. 4-ounce cans)

Topping:

1 1/3 cups sugar	10 Tbsp. butter
1 cup unsifted flour	thin powdered sugar frosting
4 tsp. cinnamon	

Scald milk. Stir in 1/2 cup sugar, salt and 1/2 cup butter. Cool to lukewarm. Measure water into large, warm bowl. Sprinkle or crumble yeast in and stir until dissolved. Add lukewarm milk mixture, egg and 2 cups flour. Beat until smooth. Stir in remaining flour to make a stiff batter. Cover tightly. Refrigerate 2 hours, or up to 2 days. Reserve apple slices.

Topping: Combine 1 1/3 cups sugar, 1 cup flour, cinnamon and 10 tablespoons butter.

Divide dough in half. On a lightly floured board roll half of dough into a 12x9-inch rectangle. Place in a 13x9x2-inch greased baking pan.

Arrange 1/2 of apple slices on dough. Sprinkle with 1/2 topping mixture. Repeat with remaining half of dough, apples and topping. Cover and let rise in warm place about 45 minutes.

Bake at 375°F. for 35 minutes or until done. Drizzle with powdered sugar frosting.

Breakfast Honey Cake
Ontbijtkoek

Mina Baker-Roelofs of Pella, Iowa

1 cup honey
1 cup brown sugar
3 cups flour
1 Tbsp. butter
1/2 cup cold water
1/2 cup milk

1/3 to 1/2 tsp. anise flavoring
1 tsp. anise seed
1/3 cup finely chopped
  almonds
1 1/2 tsp. baking soda mixed
  in 1 tsp. hot water

Mix in order given. Bake in 2 small greased loaf pans or 1 long angel food pan for 35 minutes at 350°F.

Raisin Cake
Groningse Koek

Charlotte de Blecourt says that Groningse koek *is a favorite of her Dutch immigrant husband, Jaap. "In the Netherlands it's a traditional cake served with tea and coffee in the afternoon or evening," says Charlotte. "I think it's more like a quick bread, but my husband claims it's a cake. This recipe is from my friend Ida Bakker, who came from the Netherlands the same time as my husband."*

Jaap manages Windmill Island Park in Holland, Michigan. His ancestors were French Huguenots who fled to the Netherlands during the seventeenth century. Jaap immigrated to the United States from Groningen, the Dutch province from which this cake takes its name.

1 cup sugar
1 cup water
1 cup raisins
1/2 cup margarine
1/2 to 3/4 tsp. cinnamon

1/2 tsp. ginger
1/2 tsp. cloves
2 cups flour
1/2 tsp. baking powder
1/2 tsp. baking soda

Combine sugar, water, raisins and margarine in saucepan. Boil for 2 minutes. When slightly cooled, stir in cinnamon, ginger and cloves. Cool to room temperature. Fold in flour, baking powder and baking soda. Bake in greased and floured loaf pan at 325°F. for 1 hour.

Brown Raisin Cake
Rozijnenkoek

Before immigrating to South Holland, Illinois, Edward and Winnie Niehof owned a bakery in the Netherlands.

1 15-oz. pkg. dark raisins	2 cups sugar
2 cups water	1 tsp. baking soda
1 tsp. cinnamon	1 cup hot water
1/2 tsp. nutmeg	4 cups flour
1/2 tsp. cloves	2 tsp. baking powder
2 Tbsp. shortening	

Mix raisins, water, cinnamon, nutmeg and cloves in saucepan. Bring to boil and simmer for 3 minutes. Cool. Add shortening and sugar. Dissolve baking soda in hot water and add. Sift together flour and baking powder. Add to raisin mixture. Pour into 2 greased and floured 9x5-inch loaf pans. Bake for 1 hour at 350°F.

Apple Tart
Appeltaart

Martha van Roekel Aarsen of Orange City, Iowa, remembers, "In the Netherlands during World War II, whenever we could get any apples, we would make this as a special treat." She came to America in 1955 with her husband and three sons.

1 cup butter or margarine	4 large apples
1 cup sugar	1/2 cup raisins
1 egg, separated	1 tsp. cinnamon
2 cups flour	1/2 tsp. water

Cream butter and sugar. Add egg white and stir. Add flour and knead well. Roll out half of dough and place in 9-inch round springform pan. Peel and slice apples. Arrange on dough. Sprinkle raisins and cinnamon over apples. Roll out remaining dough and cut in strips. Crisscross strips over apples and around the circumference of the pan. Blend egg yolk with water and brush over crust. Bake at 350°F. for 1 hour. Makes 12 servings.

Taai Taai

For Janni Drooger of Terrace, British Columbia, Taai Taai *is a special treat for* Sinterklaas *Day or for coffee time.*

3 cups dark corn syrup
1 cup boiling water
3 tsp. anise seed

3 1/2 cups flour, sifted
1 tsp. baking soda

Mix corn syrup, boiling water and anise seed. Cool completely. Mix flour and baking soda. Blend with syrup mixture. Pour into well-greased 12x18-inch baking dish. Bake at 300°F. for 30 minutes. Let it cool 5 minutes. Remove from pan. Cut and serve.

Dutch Apple Cake
Hollandse Appelkoek

Ann Margot Doop DeVries of Grand Rapids, Michigan, has been, for many years, a secretary for the Dutch Immigrant Society in Grand Rapids. Born in Haarlem, the Netherlands, she emigrated to the United States with her husband at the age of nineteen. This recipe is a favorite for birthday parties.

2 cups sifted flour
3 tsp. baking powder
1/2 tsp. salt
1/2 cup shortening
1 egg
Sauce:
1 cup brown sugar
1 Tbsp. flour
1 cup boiling water

3/4 cup milk
2 cups thinly sliced apples
1/3 cup sugar
1 tsp. cinnamon

1 Tbsp. butter
1 tsp. vanilla

Sift flour, baking powder and salt together. Cut in shortening as for pastry. Beat egg, add milk and stir quickly into flour mixture. Place sliced apples in greased deep 9-inch pie pan. Sprinkle with sugar and cinnamon and spread with dough. Bake at 350°F. for 45 minutes. Loosen cake from sides of pan. Cool 5 to 10 minutes. Turn out on serving plate. Serve with *bruine saus.*

To make sauce, mix sugar and flour together. Add boiling water gradually, stirring constantly. Add butter and vanilla, cooking until mixture thickens slightly. Makes 8 servings.

Ginger Butter Cake
Gemberboterkoek

Ruth Kortenhoven Brinks of Grand Rapids, Michigan, took a class in Dutch cooking during a family stay in the Netherlands. A Dutch friend from Haren, Groningen, shared this recipe with her.

2 1/4 cups flour
1 1/4 cups sugar
1 1/4 cups butter
1/2 tsp. baking powder
2 tsp. ground ginger
2 Tbsp. sliced preserved ginger

1 tsp. vanilla
3 drops lemon flavoring
pinch of salt
2 eggs
15 almonds, blanched

Grease a 9 or 10-inch round pan and dust with flour. Place all ingredients except eggs and almonds in a large bowl. Using pastry blender, cut butter into the dry ingredients until they resemble a pie crust mixture. Reserve 2 tablespoons egg white for glazing. Add eggs. Knead quickly into a ball. Do not handle excessively. Press mixture into prepared pan. Brush with reserved egg white and top with almonds. Bake at 400°F. for 45 minutes.

Dutch Apple Pie
Appeltaart

Shirely Weller of Pella, Iowa, often uses this recipe when serving a Dutch lunch to guests from out of town. Shirely's husband, Dr. Kenneth Weller, is former president of Central College in Pella.

(1) 9-inch pastry shell, unbaked
8 apples, peeled and sliced
3/4 cup sugar
1 tsp. cinnamon

2/3 cup flour
1/2 cup brown sugar
1/3 cup margarine

Mix apples, sugar and cinnamon. Pour into pie shell. Mix flour, brown sugar and margarine until crumbly. Sprinkle over apples. Bake 10 minutes at 425°F. Reduce to 375°F. Bake 30 minutes longer.

Dutch Almond Torte
Amandeltaartje

After immigrating to the United States, William and Ann Veldman worked at a variety of jobs to make ends meet. They have owned pastry shops both in the Netherlands and in California, where William's bakery talents are in demand by local restaurants and church groups.

3/4 cup butter
3/4 cup sugar
1 egg
2 cups flour

1 Tbsp. baking powder
1/4 cup milk
1/2 to 1 cup sliced almonds

Filling:
1/2 cup almond paste
1/4 cup sugar

1 egg
2 Tbsp. butter

Mix butter, sugar and egg. Add flour and baking powder. In separate bowl, mix filling ingredients. Grease and flour 8-inch cake pan or pie pan. Divide dough into two parts. Spread one part in bottom of pan. Spread filling over crust. Spread remaining dough over filling. Brush with milk. Sprinkle with sliced almonds. Bake at 375°F. for 30 minutes. Serve cold.

Almond Roll
Banketstaven

Arvella DeHaan Schuller of Garden Grove, California, bakes this tasty pastry for the Schuller family Christmas. Arvella's husband, Dr. Robert Schuller, is the well-known pastor of the Garden Grove Community Church. He appears on national television each Sunday with his "Hour of Power" broadcasts.

1 lb. almond paste
2 cups sugar
3 eggs
4 cups flour

1 lb. margarine
1 cup water
1 egg white or 1/4 cup milk

Let almond paste, sugar and eggs stand in bowl for 30 minutes.

In separate bowl cut margarine into flour. Stir in water, a few tablespoons at a time, as for pie crust. Dough may be refrigerated overnight, if desired. Divide dough into 4 equal parts. (continued)

Roll each on floured board into 13x8-inch strips. Cut each strip in half to form 13x4-inch strips.

Prepare filling by mixing almond paste, sugar and eggs. Shape into 8 cylinders 12 inches long, the diameter of a dime. Place filling rolls on length of dough. Fold over ends and then the long sides, moistening one edge to seal before pressing closed.

Place rolls with seam down on cookie sheet. Brush tops with egg white or milk. Bake at 425°F. for 10 minutes. Prick holes on top of each and return to oven. Bake 10 minutes at 375°F. or until lightly browned.

Rolls may be decorated with powdered sugar icing if desired.

Snowballs
Sneeuwballen

Phil and Jan Webber live in Pella, Iowa. They perform with the Dutch Family Singers during Pella's annual Tulip Time. Phil teaches foreign languages, including Dutch, at Central College.

In keeping with Dutch tradition, the Webbers serve Snowballs on New Year's Eve, but they add, "Snowballs are so good, we like them anytime." The Webbers often save preparation time by purchasing a commercially prepared cream puff dough instead of preparing their own.

Their final word of advice in preparing Snowballs for New Year's Eve is, "Remember that resolutions about your diet don't start until tomorrow!"

1 cup boiling water	oil or shortening for deep
1/2 cup butter	frying
1 cup flour	sweetened whipped cream
1/4 tsp. salt	powdered sugar
4 eggs	

Combine water and butter. Add flour and salt. Stir over low heat until mixture forms a ball, leaving the sides of the pan. Add eggs one at a time, beating vigorously after each addition.

Heat oil. Drop in rounded tablespoons of dough. When fully puffed and golden, remove balls and drain thoroughly. With the point of a pastry bag, make a small hole in each ball and fill with sweetened whipped cream. Roll in powdered sugar, Stack in a mound to serve. Makes 12.

Deep-Fried Doughnuts
Ollebollen

Cobie Postma of Escalon, California, follows the Dutch tradition of making oliebollen *for New Year's Eve. "In the Netherlands, many families are busy making* oliebollen *the last day of the year," says Cobie. "When we emigrated, we kept this tradition, which my family enjoys very much."*

Audrey Zwaal, who uses a similar recipe suggests serving oliebollen *with a glass of wine or spiced tea. Audrey lives in Terra Ceia, North Carolina, where a small group of Dutch people settled in 1940, clearing the land and using canals to drain the swamps, much as their ancestors had done in Holland.*

3 eggs 1/4 cup warm water
1/2 cup sugar
1/4 cup melted butter or oil
2 cups milk
4 1/2 cups flour
1 pkg. dry yeast

1 cup raisins or 2 cups diced
   apples (optional)
oil for deep frying
powdered sugar

In large mixing bowl combine eggs and sugar. Add butter or oil. Then add milk and flour. Mix the dry yeast in warm water. Add to batter. Place mixture in a warm place. Let rise for a few hours. Punch down and let rise again. Add apples or raisins if desired. Drop from teaspoons into hot oil. Deep-fry until done. Roll in powdered sugar. Makes 40 or 50.

Deep-Fried Doughnuts
Oliekoeken

Arne and Darwin Vermaat own and operate the Royal Dutch Bakery in Orange City, Iowa. Baking is a family tradition. Their father, John, was a baker and still works occasionally at the Royal Dutch Bakery.

1 cup sugar
1 egg
1 1/2 cups milk
4 cups flour

2 tsp. baking powder
1 cup raisins
1 apple, sliced
oil or fat for deep frying

Mix sugar with egg and milk. Add dry ingredients. Stir in raisins and apple slices. Drop one tablespoonful at a time into deep hot fat. Fry until done. Makes 3 dozen.

Pennsylvania Dutchies

Arne Vermaat owns the Royal Dutch Bakery in Orange City, Iowa.

4 tsp. baking powder	1 1-ounce cake yeast
2 1/2 cups flour	1 cup + 2 Tbsp. water
1 3/4 cups cake flour	1 large egg
2 Tbsp. sugar	1 1/2 cup raisins
1/2 tsp. salt	sugar or confectioners' sugar
1/4 cup powdered milk	(powdered sugar) glaze
6 Tbsp. shortening	oil for deep-fat frying

Sift baking powder with flour. Stir in dry ingredients. Cut in shortening. Dissolve yeast in lukewarm water. Mix together all ingredients except raisins. Let set 10 minutes. Roll out dough to 1/2-inch thickness. Apply raisins to half the dough. Fold other half over the raisined half. Roll out to 1/4-inch thickness. Cut into rectangles approximately 2 3/4 x 4 3/4 inches. Place in deep fat fryer immediately at 375°F. Turn once till both sides are a golden dark brown. Finish by rolling in sugar or a glaze while still hot. Makes approximately 75-80.

Note: Arne says *Pennsylvania Dutchies* freeze well in the dough stage. To serve just thaw and fry.

Fruit Soup
Vruchtensiroop

Eleanor Zylstra Lieuwen of New Holland, South Dakota, a former home economics teacher, doubles this recipe to make 5 quarts of fruit soup for a Dutch smorgasbord each October.

2 qts. water	1 cup pearl tapioca
1 cup raisins	1/8 tsp. cloves
1 cup prunes	1/8 tsp. cinnamon
1 apple, diced	1 cup apple juice
1/2 lb. dried apricots	1 cup wine
1 cup brown sugar	juice of 1 lemon

Place water, fruits, brown sugar, tapioca and spices in heavy saucepan and simmer until tender (about 30 minutes). Stir in apple juice. Cool. Add wine and lemon juice. Serve warm or chilled.

Buttercake

This recipe from Emma Van Hoek of Denver, Colorado, is prepared in large quantities for sale at the Bethesda Dutch Festival and is a very popular item.

1/2 cup (1 stick) butter
1/2 cup (1 stick) margarine
1 scant cup sugar
2 cups flour

2 tsp. almond flavoring
1/4 cup cream
1/2 cup almond slices

Knead together butter, margarine, sugar, flour and almond flavoring until well-blended and soft. Pat mixture into two pie tins. Brush with cream and decorate with almond slices. Bake at 375°F. for 15 to 20 minutes, until slightly brown on edges. Centers should be soft. Do not overbake. Freezes well and can be kept frozen for months.

Note: Emma says 2 sticks of butter O.K. instead of one each of butter and margarine.

Filled Buttercake

Tina Vanderkwaak, Chilliwack, British Columbia

Dough:
2 cups flour
1 cup butter
1 cup sugar

1 egg
pinch of salt

Filling:
2 cups blanched almonds
1/4 cup sugar

1 small egg, beaten
peel of 1/2 lemon, grated

Knead all the ingredients for dough into a firm ball. Divide the dough in half. Press one half into a buttered 8-inch pie pan.

Grind almonds. Mix with sugar, beaten egg and grated lemon peel and grind once more. Place filling on top of dough in pan and cover with second half of dough. Bake at 350°F. for 1 hour, until golden brown. Remove from pan and cool on wire rack. Slice into wedges to serve.

Dutch Apple Fritters
Hollandse Appelflappen

Jean Van Vossen Strong of Oak Forest, Illinois, is assistant curator at the Dutch Heritage Center of Trinity Christian College. She writes that apple fritters are a traditional holiday specialty.

6 large cooking apples	1 egg, beaten
1 cup flour	1/2 cup milk
2 tsp. baking powder	oil for deep frying
1/4 tsp. salt	powdered sugar
1 Tbsp. sugar	

Peel and core apples and slice into 1/3-inch thick slices. Combine dry ingredients. Add egg and milk and mix well for 3 minutes. Dip apple slices in batter and deep-fry in hot oil until golden. Sprinkle with powdered sugar.

Rusk Pancakes

Mina Baker-Roelofs likes this recipe from the Netherlands National Tourist Office. She says, "The procedure is similar to making French toast, but you use Dutch rusks instead."

2 eggs	4 Dutch rusks
2 tsp. sugar	1 Tbsp. butter or margarine
1/2 tsp. vanilla	powdered sugar
1 cup milk, lukewarm	

Beat eggs with sugar and vanilla. Slowly add lukewarm milk. Dip rusks into mixture (time allowed for dipping will determine amount of liquid absorbed). Brown both sides of rusks in skillet in which butter has been melted. Turn rusks carefully to prevent breaking. Serve with powdered sugar.

Mina says, "Rusk pancakes are also good with syrup, but that's an American innovation. The Dutch use powdered sugar."

Garden Remedies

According to the New York State Office of Parks, Recreation and Historic Preservation, Albany doctors in the 1740s used herbs to treat illness. Herbs grown today in the gardens of the Schuyler Mansion and Fort Crailo of Albany are examples of those used in the 1600s and 1700s to combat illness. Some of the herbs and their uses are:

rue: to counteract poisons, tonic for colic, headache.

lady's mantle: soothing effect on nerves, sore throats, sore joints and toothache.

tarragon: increase stamina.

chives: aid digestion of fatty foods.

thyme: strong antiseptic.

yarrow: believed to strengthen the medicinal powers of other plants; also an herb for wounds, and a general tonic.

dill: sedative tea, help cure ulcers, ease swelling.

majoram: as a tea, for asthma.

lavender: sooth nerves and sore joints.

salad burnett: protection againt disease, healer of wounds.

sage: stomach disorders, treatment for snake bite, colds, fever; one of the most widely used herbs of the 19th century.

marigolds: herbal tea for colds.

And then there are these from the Historic Cherry Hills book, *Selected Receipts of a Van Rensselaer Family, 1785–1835. [sic]*

catnip: "stampt very fine, often apply'd to the bite of a snake; it is an Indian cure."

For a cough: "1 teacup maple sugar, the same quantity of vinegar, 1 teacup hony boilt to a syrup — one tsp at a time."